10 Sermons I Never Preached

by

Gregory Mark Schroeder

© 2011 by Gregory M. Schroeder

All rights reserved. Copyright under Berne Copyright Convention, Universal Copyright Convention, and Pan-American Copyright Convention. No part of this book may be reproduced, stored in a retrieval system, or transmitted in any form, or by any means, electronic, mechanical, photocopying, recording or otherwise, without prior permission of the author.

All scripture quotations, unless otherwise indicated, are taken from the Holy Bible, New International Version®, NIV®. Copyright ©1973, 1978, 1984, 2011 by Biblica, Inc.™ Used by permission of Zondervan. www.zondervan.com The "NIV" and "New International Version" are trademarks registered in the United States Patent and Trademark Office by Biblica, Inc.™

Library of Congress Control Number: 2013908859

ISBN 978-1484810507

IntegroWellness, Vancouver, British Columbia
For information about booking the author to speak at your event email info@integrowellness.com

Cover Photo by Alissa Pashko

Table of Contents

Introduction 4

Notes to the Reader 7

1. Inspired Weakness 10

2. Immoral Faith 24

3. Even God Doesn't Love The Ones He Should ..40

4. Integrity For Failures 63

5. Post-Moral Man 88

6. Friend Of Sinners..107

7. Shaking The Dust Off 130

8. God's Guidebook For Cynics 148

9. Saved From Everything But Ourselves 171

10. End With Hope 195

Afterword..220

Introduction

These are the ten sermons I never preached. I couldn't have. It was impossible to see what I say here while I was standing there. Then, after twenty years as a minister, I fell.

My first pulpit was an overturned apple-box in the side yard of the parsonage. I was three years old and our family lived in an apartment built on the back of the church. I began preaching for real in Bible College. I spoke on short notice. The snow of big drifts smashed up over the hood of my old Chevrolet as I plowed toward small town Saskatchewan churches with my notes spread over the dashboard. I preached in the largest church in my denomination when I was twenty-three and pastored my first congregation at twenty-five. I devoted fifteen hours every week to study and preparation. I loved preaching.

For the next twenty years I spoke from the Bible. I preached systematically through the books of the Bible one section at a time. I asked people what their big questions were in life. *How will I make payroll this month? How can I keep from stuffing my mother-in-law in the trunk? What do my kids really need to know to live well? How do I know I can trust God?* I scoured the Bible for answers. By the time I was forty-five I had preached through every one of the sixty-six books of the Bible and spoken topically hundreds of times. I had preached on four continents, preached to two people in a cold sanctuary and to thousands in a soccer stadium. I spoke in homeless shelters and at denominational conferences.

Then I burned out. After four months of sabbatical the door I had walked out for a rest closed behind me. I lost my job. A few months after that another door opened and I had an affair.

Einstein imagined the story of two men and a train. The first man stood at an open window inside the moving train and dropped a stone. As he watched the stone it fell straight down. The second man stood on the bank beside the moving train. As he watched, the stone fell in a parabolic arc. Though they both accurately saw the same thing, each man saw it differently.

I see things differently now. I am seeing things from a perspective I could not have had until I tumbled from the train. I am seeing things from the vantage point of almost everyone I had been preaching to: the fallen.

After my fall it was increasingly difficult to find myself in the moral imperatives of the Bible. However, I did recognize myself in the ironic stories of the saints and their unlikely friendships with God.

When Einstein conceived his theory of relativity (and wrote it in a four page letter to a friend!) it did not negate the cause and effect physics of Newton. Einstein's equations fulfilled Newton's and transcended them. Einstein gave us the bigger picture. Jesus said something similar about his teaching and the religious laws that had been taught until then.[1]

I still believe the sermons I preached for twenty-five years encouraging people to a good life were true, but I needed something truer.

Six years after leaving the church I studied Italian in a classroom near the centre of Rome. Across the alley bells began their song.

Do fa fa la so fa fa...

In just seven notes I was transported back to a childhood Sunday School class. I hummed softly.

---

[1] Matthew 5:17

The Lord is my Shepherd
I'll walk with him always
He leads by still waters
I'll walk with him always…

The bells were pure and bright and louder than anything we might have said in class. As the last peal faded the instructor taught another rule of grammar. I asked about an exception.

"Gregory," she said, "the rules of grammar were not made before anyone began to speak. Linguists listened to how people already spoke and wrote and then they constructed the rules of grammar to describe the language as best they could. Of course there were irregularities."

Theology is like grammar. There is no pre-ordained set of rules God lives by. Theology is a list of observations that people believe describes who God is and how he acts. There are irregularities.

In our longing for security we have put God in the box of predictable expectations. God does not live there. He may be faithful, but he is not predictable. Once my own box had been shattered by failures and truths that could not be contained, I looked again.

These are the ten sermons I never preached.

Notes to the Reader

The Bible, (literally, "the Books"), is a collection of sixty-six books written over sixteen hundred years. Evangelical Christians believe this collection of books was inspired by God, written down as the authors were carried along by the Spirit of God, and inerrant as originally given. It has been copied with rigorous accuracy over time. Evangelicals use the Bible as the authoritative guide for life and faith. Quotations, unless noted differently, are from the New International Version of the Bible.

Test everything here and keep what is good. The best truths are self-evident. Not that we discover them for ourselves, but once we learn them, we know them for ourselves, not on another's authority. A teacher taught me that 2+2=4. But I know it for myself now. The best truths, and all spiritual truths, are like that.

All names, except the author's, have been changed. Some details have been changed to respect people's privacy.

Where the author has paraphrased biblical dialogue it is indicated in the footnote.

I have run the stories of the Bible through my fingers like prayer beads and found my own interspersed like a seventh bead of a differing kind but strung on the same thread. My stories are not in chronological order, and while they might illustrate, they do not interpret the Bible. May you find your own stories here.

For those who were with me in the difficult days.

1. Inspired Weakness

*You don't have to be perfect to fulfill God's purpose.
Sometimes it helps if you are not.*

How could a man powerful enough to kill a lion or tear city gates from their walls be too weak to control himself? Samson was the strongest man in the world, but he lacked the strength that mattered most—character. If only he could have got it right. That summarizes what I heard, believed and preached for forty-five years.

I myself was burnt out. An eight month sabbatical began in January but I was finished with the church and with preaching by May. I knew I no longer fit the way I had. I was told I no longer fit at all. Did anything I'd said and done really make a difference? I was demoralized. Then, shortly before Christmas, friends invited me to Cairo.

1...

A week after arriving in Egypt we drove through Garbage City to get to the Cave Church of Cairo. Though it was a cool day, the woman in the back seat began to retch as her husband drove us through the pinched and rutted streets. She splashed perfume on a tissue and held it over her nose.

Families hauled trash into their homes to be sifted and sorted before leaving as something of recycled value. Food was eaten. Clothing worn. Metal and plastics were bundled and hauled out on the same carts that had been drawn in by donkeys with their heads down and whips to their backs. The pigs ate what no one else could stomach. Five blocks in there was a faded Coptic cross fifteen feet up the side of a building. It was the sign to turn right.

The Cave Church was discovered, or rediscovered, in the roots of Mokattam Mountain in 1974. Now it is home to a congregation of thousands of souls. Most of the parishioners walk up the road from Garbage City. A few drive from elsewhere in their Mercedes Benz, but not many.

The original sanctuary is more than a hundred metres long and fifty wide and the floor has been sloped to produce an amphitheatre of rock. The ceiling hovers fifteen metres above, and I wondered about stability in a place prone to tremors.

The walls of the cave were filled with murals sculpted in stone. The first tells of the miracle of Mokattam Mountain. Towards the end of the tenth century, Al-Muiz Li Din-Illah was the caliph in Cairo. He brought together Muslim, Christian and Jewish religious leaders to debate, with the stipulation that there should be no rancor, and with the promise of freedom so each could speak openly. Of course there was rancor, and eventually a Muslim minister of state, who had had a political conversion from Judaism, became so angry over an affront that he devised a strategy to obtain revenge.

Quoting Christ who said that if one had faith he could say to a mountain "Move" and it would, the offended minister went to the caliph and contested that the Christians should be expected to prove this. The caliph agreed and afforded the Christians four options:

1. The Christians could fulfill the scriptures and move the eastern part of Mokattam Mountain (which happened to be blocking the caliph's otherwise excellent view).
2. They could convert to Islam.
3. They could leave Egypt as exiles.
4. The Christians could be put to the sword and summarily killed.

Sometimes life is like that. The only option that doesn't mean death to some part of our life requires a miracle that is, by definition, beyond us. I needed a miracle too.

The Patriarch, as leader of the Christians, asked for three days of respite. Then he would answer. For the next three days, the Christians fasted and prayed. On the third day, while dozing, at dawn, the Patriarch saw the Virgin Mary who told him to watch for a one-eyed man carrying a jug of water near the gate. This man would bring a miracle. The man was Samaan the tanner, a shoemaker.

One day, while gripping his awl and working his trade, Samaan glimpsed the leg of a beautiful woman. Taking literally the biblical injunction to gouge out your right eye if it causes you to lust, he did. This made others think of Samaan as a holy man. His service to the poor and the sick only enhanced that perspective. Samaan, with his one eye, did not see himself that way.

When the patriarch found Samaan, and told him of the Christian's predicament and of Mary's message, the shoemaker replied, "Forgive me my father, for I am but a sinful man."

Nonetheless, in obedience, Samaan directed the patriarch to go to the mountain with the other leaders of the church, and with the caliph and his retinue. Once there, the Christians were to cry out *Kyrie Eleison—Have mercy, Lord*, four hundred times, one hundred times to each point of the compass. I can understand how a sinful man might suggest such words. There are some questions only the broken can answer.

At the end of each hundred *Have mercy*, the Christians stood, praising God, and each time they stood, the mountain rose too!

This is the miracle depicted in the first mural on the walls of the cave church: the Christians on one side, the ruler and his entourage on the other, and the risen mountain with the sun shining beneath its base.

The next mural is the image of Saint Samaan carved in stone; a splash of red paint highlighting his lost right eye, but his other eye still faces the revealed leg of the beautiful woman on his left. Every mural after that is a scene of sexual temptation. Samson and Delilah (and subsequently Samson with both his eyes gouged out). Joseph fleeing from Potiphar's wife. The woman caught in adultery. It was a curious mix of the glorious and the profane. As I contemplated the collage of images, a draft blew through the open door and scented the sanctuary with the smell of Garbage City. Life is messy. My life was messy. I was having an affair.

I met Mira on a school field trip at the beginning of my sabbatical. We never saw each other again until I left the church, then we bumped into each other everywhere. Across the island at the gas station. In a coffee shop. The same aisle in a drugstore. Then we chose to see each other. For months we talked. After twenty-three years of faithfulness I was slipping.

I talked to a therapist. "How can I stop myself?"

Not long before leaving for Egypt I chose intimacy.

No one knew. A month after Cairo my lover and I were discovered. A year later I lost the sight in my left eye.

2…

Everyone knew about Samson. Samson's mother was sterile, and, as for every barren woman in the Bible, God showed up with the promise of a child. He also gave some directions.[2]

The mother was to have no wine or other alcohol and no unclean food. No razor was to be used on the boy's head, because he was to be a Nazirite, set apart to God from birth. While a Nazirite was set apart (*nazir*) for God, they were also set apart from the fruit of the vine, including wine; corpses and anything that contained them; and cutting the hair on one's head.

The heavenly messenger added that Samson would begin the deliverance of Israel from the hands of the Philistines after forty years of oppression.

Samson's soon-to-be father realized that not only having, but raising the child was beyond their ability and asked

---

[2] Judges 13:1-24

God to send the messenger back with some insights. The Angel of the Lord returned and said the same thing again.

When the parents requested the messenger's name, he said, "Why do you ask my name? It is beyond understanding."[3]

I had never practically considered that anything in life was beyond understanding before my moral failure. Yes, I knew God's ways were higher than ours, but I reasoned that was a problem of perspective that would be remedied with time or in eternity. While the incremental creep of relaxed morals was something I guarded against, it never occurred to me that the pursuit of perfection and attempts to make sense of everything were a sure road to disaster.

"Don't be over-righteous, neither be over-wise," the teacher said in Ecclesiastes. "Why destroy yourself?"[4]

We keep trying. Even as I write this, I am trying to make some new sense of things.

Samson's parents offered a meal to the strange messenger but the Angel of the Lord refused to eat the food, suggested an offering to God, and ascended in the flames. The father thought they were good as dead for looking into the face of God, but the mother reasoned that if God wanted to kill them, he wouldn't have bothered with the instructions. They'd already be dead. Practical woman.

Here are the highlights of Samson's compelling and tragic morality tale:[5]

The boy was born and grew and the Lord blessed Samson, and the Spirit of the Lord began to stir him. The very next verse of the Bible says Samson went down to Timna and found a young Philistine woman he wanted for a wife. Marrying outside the chosen people of Israel was unacceptable. Marrying one of the enemy must have been even worse for Samson's parents.

---

[3] Judges 13:18
[4] Ecclesiastes 7:16
[5] Judges 13:1-16:30

The next time the Spirit of the Lord came powerfully on Samson as he and his parents were approaching the vineyards of Timna on the way to see the young woman. A young lion roared towards Samson and he tore it apart with his bare hands! Apparently his parents didn't see what happened, and Samson didn't tell them. Later, when Samson went back to marry the young woman from Timna, he found a swarm of bees nested in the carcass of the lion and he scooped out honey for himself and gave some to his parents too. But he never told them it came from a dead body.

At the beginning of the week-long wedding feast Samson told a riddle to the thirty companions assigned to him.

> Out of the eater, something to eat;
> out of the strong, something sweet.[6]

If the companions solved the riddle within the week, Samson would give them thirty linen garments and thirty sets of clothes. If they could not, they had to give him the same. Three days passed and the companions had no clue, so they went to Samson's bride and threatened to burn her and her family to death if she did not tell.

But she didn't know. She pled with Samson, sobbing that he must not really love her since he had shared something with her people that he kept from her. What could be worse than a weepy bride? Samson told her the story, she told his companions, they solved the riddle, and Samson realized what had happened.

The Spirit of God came on Samson with power just then. He went to Ashkelon, struck down thirty men and stripped them of their clothes and gave them to those who had answered his riddle. Hot with anger, Samson went back to his father's home and in his absence his wife was given to a

---

[6] Judges 14:14

friend from the wedding. Samson cooled down and went back to be with his wife, but discovered she was no longer his.

"This time I have a right to get even,"[7] he said.

He tied torches to the tails of foxes and set them loose in the fields of the Philistines. He burnt everything to ashes—the grain, the vineyards, even the olive trees. Imagine losing every source of income and sustenance. When Samson's enemies discovered who had done this, they burned the woman and her father to death.

When someone loses too much of what is important to them, they lose something of themselves too. When we lose something we care about deeply, we sometimes lose the ability to care. Samson lost his bride and viciously attacked his enemies and slaughtered many of them. He took his revenge. Then, he waited in a cave. Whatever others did to me when I lost my vocation and my community, I did worse when I betrayed my wife. *Why don't I care more?* I wondered.

The Philistines came for their revenge and asked the Israelites where Samson was. The Philistines were masters of the Israelites, and while Samson's countrymen may not have wanted to turn him over, neither did they want to suffer. Samson agreed to let them tie him up and turn him over if only they promised not to kill him. Then, when the Philistines were shouting and coming toward him, the Spirit of God came powerfully on Samson.

The ropes that bound Samson became like the burnt wick of a candle and fell from his hands. Samson picked up the jawbone of a dead donkey and with it he slew a thousand Philistines.

"With a donkey's jawbone,
I have made donkeys of them."[8] Samson said.
Then he threw the jawbone away.

---

[7] Judges 15:3
[8] Judges 15:16

Samson wasn't to touch anything dead. Are there times when we accomplish God's purpose with something outside the boundaries? Does it make a difference? Does it make it better if we discard that thing once it has served its purpose?

After twenty years of leading Israel, Samson went to Gaza and slept with a prostitute. The men of the city were waiting for dawn to kill him, but Samson left in the middle of the night. He tore the city gates, posts and all from the walls, and set them on a hill looking to Hebron, the place where Abraham, the friend of God, had first settled in the Promised Land. Curiously, that is the first time in the story that Samson performed a feat of strength without any mention of the Spirit of the Lord coming on him.

Samson means light. At this point in the story, he fell in love with a woman named Delilah. She did not fall in love with him. Delilah means darkness. When the Philistine rulers came to Delilah and offered a fortune for the secret of Samson's strength, she agreed. Three times she tried to find his secret and three times she failed. What she could not accomplish through cunning or seduction she got another way. She poked and nagged at Samson until he was tired to death. Samson told her his long hair was the key to his strength.

Weariness is the root of all kinds of failure. In a culture where hard work is high virtue, the best workers may be the most vulnerable to the failures that are not a sign of bad character, but simply exhaustion.

While Samson slept in Delilah's lap, a barber shaved his head. When she cried out that the Philistines were upon him he rose to fight, but he was unaware that the Lord had left him.

I could cry for that phrase. I was tired to death too.

Six years after planting a church that was in the top two percent for Canadian growth rates, I had thyroid cancer. It wasn't the sort that kills many, but it wearied me. The thyroid controls the body's metabolism and when that regulator between my head and my heart was removed I lost my strength. I could no longer think clearly. My memory was sporadic. My willpower was diminished. I was often tired and cold. I hoped for a sabbatical, but it didn't work out, so I pressed on. Sometimes a lack of faith is nothing more than weariness.

Over the next six years the church grew more, and like a wick without wax, I burned down. Eventually I took my sabbatical. But they didn't want me back. I get that now. It's hard to follow a leader who has run out of both energy and humour. *Did nothing I said make any difference?* I felt dead.

Then I met someone who made me feel alive.

Nine months after leaving my wife the retina detached in my left eye. After the second operation I woke to discover the lens within my eye was gone. Life was a blur on that side. First I wore a patch, then my mind shut out the images.

Samson's enemies came upon him but he didn't know his strength was gone.[9] Before he knew anything else, his eyes were gouged out and his hands were shackled. He was set to a grindstone in prison. He may not have been seeing clearly for a while, but now he was blind, incapable, and enslaved.

The Philistines celebrated. They thanked their god Dagon for their victory over Samson, and while they were worshipping, Samson was brought out to perform for them. His strength had been reduced to a party trick. Samson asked the servant who led him to put his hands on the pillars that supported the temple. Thousands were crowded inside. Thousands more were on the roof.

> Sovereign LORD, remember me. Please, God, strengthen me just once more, and let me with one blow get revenge on the Philistines for my two eyes… Let me die with the Philistines.[10]

---

[9] Judges 16:20ff
[10] Judges 16:28-30

Why would God answer a prayer like that?

Standing between the two main pillars Samson pushed with all his might and the place came down.

3...

Ten years ago I would have preached about the dangers of a vengeful spirit. (*I only did to them what they did to me.*) I'd have said that bitterness and rage blind us, and an unforgiving spirit shackles us to those who have wronged us. I'd have said that when we flirt with trouble we are courting disaster. I still believe those things.

But something else is happening in this story. There are odd currents in the life of Samson.

While the inevitable consequences of life rolled over Samson like they roll over all of us, why didn't Samson's neglect of his vows have any early consequences? He scooped honey from a dead carcass he wasn't supposed to touch, and gave some to his mother too (she wasn't to touch anything from the dead either). Even from the dead glories of life we sometimes draw something sweet.

He slept with a prostitute and none of his strength was diminished. It is not just that he didn't lose strength because of his failures, God actually empowered him with his Spirit to do many of those things. Before Samson chose a Philistine wife the Spirit stirred him. Before he beat up thirty men and stripped them of their clothes because he had to pay up on a lost bet, the Spirit of the Lord came on him powerfully. The Spirit empowered him again and Samson picked up the jaw of a dead donkey and destroyed his enemies. After dropping the dry bone he called out to God in his thirst and God split the earth so water flowed out.

If God is in the details, he doesn't seem overly concerned about them in the story of Samson. Why?

In July 1799, French soldiers were strengthening the defenses of Fort Julien, near the Egyptian port city of Rashid, or, as the Europeans called it, Rosetta, when they discovered a slab of stone with three inscriptions on one face. The third inscription was in Greek, but the first was in hieroglyphs, the ancient Egyptian symbols whose meaning had been lost before the fall of the Roman Empire. Some surmised that all three languages held the same message, and by working from the Greek inscription that could be translated, scholars came to understand Egyptian hieroglyphs.

There is a Rosetta Stone in the biblical story of Samson that brings understanding to the strongman's life and message. Just after the Spirit of the Lord began to stir Samson for the first time he wanted badly to marry a girl from the wrong neighborhood.

"She's the right one for me."[11] he said.

His parents were appalled at the idea, but the Bible says, "His parents did not know this was from the Lord."[12]

Odd, odd, odd. The book goes on to say the Lord "was seeking an occasion to confront the Philistines."[13] That is the Rosetta Stone that interprets the life of Samson. If God's purpose for Samson was to confront the Philistines, Samson's life was a raging success! He provoked them with his intended wedding to a Philistine woman. The tension built with the riddle from the dead lion and escalated with his beating of the thirty men whose clothes he took. When his wife was given to another he burned their fields to ashes. Then the woman he loved was burned to death. Every act of revenge was amplified. Did Samson's grief and rage prompt him to fulfill his calling? Was God angering Samson on purpose?

The Philistines came to kill Samson after he slept with a prostitute, but he woke and took their gates, the symbols of security, commerce and justice, and hauled them away to the birthplace of his own nation. The next time the Philistines

---

[11] Judges 14:3
[12] Judges 14:4
[13] Judges 14:4

came for him Samson killed a thousand of them. If confrontation was Samson's goal, he was on a roll.

Even Samson's death can be seen differently viewed through God's purpose for his life. That Samson accomplished more of his purpose in his death than he did in all of his life might even be an accolade.

Questions remain. If God didn't take his Spirit away when Samson married outside the covenant, when he touched something dead, when he slept with prostitutes or fell in love with a dark woman, why did God's Spirit leave Samson when his hair was cut? Was that simply the last thread to be cut in an unraveling life?

Was Samson's hair the outward sign of an inward reality? Did he lose his strength then because he believed he would? Probably not. He didn't know the Spirit of the Lord had left him. In the moral economy there are some failures that cost a great deal and contribute nothing. Are we still responsible for our failures even if God has moved us in that direction? Is God? Does it matter?

Samson's hair began to grow. The Rabbis say that if a Nazirite breaks his vow he can shave his head and make a fresh start. Though it's hard to understand how doing the thing you're not supposed to gives you a fresh start, everyone needs a clause like that.

Samson's hair began to grow again, and his strength grew with it. Though the strength of it may be lost for a time, the gift and calling of our lives never is. The Apostle Paul said they are irrevocable.[14]

If I were to preach again, I would spend less time telling people how to get it right, and more time offering insights on how to make the most of what they have been given.

Many, many years later Samson is mentioned in the biblical hall of fame as one of those "whose weakness was

---

[14] Romans 11:29

turned to strength; and who became powerful in battle and routed foreign armies."[15] Was it that Samson became strong where he had once been weak? Or that his weakness was used for strength? Certainly the latter. Probably both.

After my cancerous thyroid was surgically removed (seven years before I was removed from the church) I went to the Mayo Clinic in Scottsdale Arizona for radiation treatment. A technician led me to a room where a lead box waited on a table. A lid with a prominent handle sat on top.

"When I have left the room I want you to take the lid off the box and drink the cup inside," the technician said. "Can you do that?"

"I can" I said.

"You'll do the same dose tomorrow, and for the next week you need to stay more than three meters away from pregnant women and flush the toilet twice."

After the radioactive drink I walked across the parking lot to my hotel. The Arizona air shimmered over the pavement and beyond that the arms of cacti reached for the sun. I changed into my bathing suit and went to the pool. An older man with a Marine tattoo unearthed bits of his life and I inevitably turned things to religion.

When I spoke of God's unconditional grace, the man asked, "What's the worst thing you've ever done?"

I knew the question was crucial, but I couldn't think of a deserving answer. I tried to kick-start the conversation again, but it was dead.

Ten years later the man who would replace me at church asked the same question. "What is the worst thing you've ever done?"

He asked for a different reason but I still lacked a real answer. I understood grace intellectually then. That's like a person with no sense of smell or taste saying they appreciate

---

[15] Hebrews 11:32-34

food. They may have chewed and swallowed, but it's not the same.

In the year after my fall I met my lover's friends.

"So you're a minister?" they often asked. They all knew what I had done.

I took it as a rebuke and usually replied that I had been a minister but no longer was. Finally, after I'd been asked for the fifth or sixth time and had denied my vocation, a man said to me, "Too bad. I was hoping for someone to talk with about spiritual things."

God is at work in more than our goodness. Failure creates a whole new kind of strength.

2. Immoral Faith

You don't have to be good to believe in God. Faith trumps morality.

1...

God asked Abraham to kill his son.[16] While there are some anguished but conceivable reasons for killing one's own child, none of them applied to Abraham. Isaac, the divinely promised child, did nothing deserving of death. He was not to be killed so others would be delivered from his evil. Neither was he to be altruistically sacrificed like a son marching off to war so others might live. The foreshadowing of God's sacrifice of his own son is a great literary device but there's more going on here.

When God told Abraham to sacrifice the boy, God didn't give a reason. God wanted something more than ethics from Abraham.

Abraham and his son Isaac set out right away. The boy carried the wood for the sacrificial flames and his father carried a knife and the fire.

"Where is the sacrifice?"[17] Isaac asked.

"God will provide,"[18] his father answered.

At the critical moment, on the same mountain where God's son Jesus would die,[19] Abraham lifted the knife. The boy looked up, and God only knew that Abraham would do *anything* for Him. The boy knew it too and after that referred

---

[16] Genesis 22:1-12
[17] Genesis 22:7 author's paraphrase
[18] Genesis 22:8
[19] 2 Chronicles 3:1 says that the Temple was built on Mount Moriah, the same mountain Abraham was directed to, the same region, or perhaps even hilltop, where Christ was crucified.

to God as *"The Fear"*.[20]

I lived with *Fear and Trembling* for twenty-five years. The dilemma of Soren Kierkegaard's book by that name tugged and twisted at the edges of my convictions as I pondered the fact that God asked Abraham to kill his son. I was introduced to the book by my favorite Bible school professor in a class on Contemporary Theology. The professor would later become the president of the denomination and would lose his own son to a drunk driver. He lost a daughter too.

God stopped Abraham in the backswing before the knife actually finished the boy off. Kierkegaard's point in *Fear and Trembling*, the truth I tried to unravel for twenty-five years, was that God asked Abraham to do something immoral and hoped he would! God was looking for something that transcended ethics in Abraham and took his willingness to sacrifice his son as a sign of his faith in God. Abraham loved God, feared God, trusted God, more than the rules,[21] and God accounted that to Abraham as righteousness.

"A person is justified by faith apart from the works of the law."[22]

Today we would call the authorities, report the madman and have him locked up. Instead, Abraham became the father of faith.

Some say that God never planned to go through with it. God may not have ever intended for Isaac to die, but Abraham thought he did, believed he did. That is exactly why Abraham's faith was counted as righteousness. God saw Abraham as a righteous man precisely because he was willing

---

[20] Genesis 31:42,53
[21] Genesis 22:12
[22] Romans 3:28

to do the worst thing imaginable and the Bible holds him up as the prime example of faith. It's hard to keep one foot in that boat while the other is on the dock of ethical absolutes.

We learned other things in that Contemporary Theology class. We studied the liberal theology of Germans like Bultmann, Tillich and Niebuhr and tore them apart for their logical inconsistencies. I was certain of everything in those days. I hadn't seen enough of either life or the world to understand real suffering.

I wrote a paper based on the law of non-contradiction (If A?B and B=C then A?C) that ravaged oriental philosophy (in my own mind at least). My professor loved it. When he showed it to an Asian colleague the man said it would mean nothing to a Daoist. Figures. The argument only worked if you thought life was logical.

It never occurred to us that other cultures and minds might have known something we did not. I never thought to ask *Why would these people write these things?* It never occurred to me to wonder what other cultures knew about suffering and the meaning of life.

There is a Rabbinic tradition that says Sarah and Abraham were estranged after he almost killed the boy she waited ninety years for. After the near-sacrifice Abraham went and stayed in Beersheba. Sarah was in Hebron. If Isaac's birth announcement in their old age was a joke that Sarah got (Sarah laughed when God said she'd give birth, and she then named the baby Isaac, which means "laughter"), Isaac's near-death experience was no laughing matter. Abraham returned after Sarah's death and mourned her.[23]

---

[23] Genesis 22:19, 23:2

The sacrifices we make for God have real consequences.

You don't hear about this much, but if you have lived with the idea that your sacrifices for God will come without cost you are mistaken. Jesus talked about cutting off a hand or gouging out an eye to keep oneself from sinning. I have lived without sight long enough to stumble.

Months after leaving my wife my retina detached in my right eye. It detached again and I lost most of my vision in that eye. While my loss was not from obedience, the costs were vivid. When I lived without any functional sight in one eye my balance and depth were skewed. Abraham showed God he loved Him more than anything, yet his son called God *"The Fear"* and the woman he had fallen instantly, deeply and lastingly in love with did not live in the same city when she died.

The darkness of detached retinas and blurred spiritual vision led me to a new clarity, but there have been times when I sat in the dark without friends, community, or family. There are real costs when we follow God, even if we do not follow cleanly.

2...

I was fifteen and Claire was thirteen when she walked into church for the first time. I fell instantly in love with her. Her parents had converted from Catholicism (that was how we saw it) and brought their six children with them in the exodus.

At the end of our first real date we parked at the base of Knox Mountain and after one brush of our lips we talked until three in the morning. When I got home I was drawn to the light of my parent's room like a moth to flame. They were propped against the headboard, reading.

"I guess I blew it, eh?" I said.

I will never forget my father's response. "If you never made mistakes we wouldn't know we had given you all the responsibility we could have."

"So...?" I asked.

"We'll pull you back if it becomes a problem."

I called Claire's dad the next day and apologized.

He didn't like the idea of anyone dating his daughter. Occasionally he relented. This went on and off throughout high school and by the end I was aware enough to see it was troubling her.

One day I prayed, *If this is going to hurt her, let her lose her affection for me.*

A week later she told me she wanted to "just be friends." It was a terrible answer to prayer. How could I have known it is impossible to love without hurting and being hurt?

After ten years of absence, I encountered Claire in the basement of the seminary I attended hoping to strengthen my character to biblical proportions. It was a musty place with unsealed foundations that jutted up unpredictably above the edges of the floor. Cracks in the concrete had been patched to keep water from seeping in, but the whole building was to be demolished in six months. The space was cluttered with an assortment of low tables and old couches that exhaled the scents of the past whenever someone settled onto the cushions.

Claire walked past with a classmate of mine. I wasn't certain if it was her, but she returned a few seconds later.

"Greg?" she queried with the familiar tilt of her head and tone of voice.

"It's been too long," I replied predictably, but honestly.

She lowered herself into the loveseat across from me while the classmate of mine occupied the other end. She introduced her companion and he moved a little closer to her, and then settled back into his corner as I assured her that we were already acquainted.

The next hour jumped by as the conversation flowed from what we were doing now to how we had felt the first time we met. She was in the travel industry, and still single. I was completing a Master's Degree and was well married with two children.

We recalled being teens when I was a carpenter's helper on the renovation of her father's house. At the end of one day Claire had challenged me to a game of twenty-one on the patio.

"I felt awkward and un-athletic," she said then in the college basement.

"I thought you were elegant. I felt sweaty and dirty."

"I thought you were rugged!"

We laughed and enjoyed the feelings from the distance memory gives. When the time came to go, we parted with warmth, but without expectations.

The following day I bumped into her friend again in a hallway between classes. He was a tall man.

"I wouldn't have guessed that you knew Claire," I said and looked up just a bit into his face.

"We were engaged," he said flatly.

"I never knew," I continued. "She's a wonderful person."

I moved back a bit.

"When is the date?" I asked, trying to move the conversation to less awkward terrain.

"It's not. We broke it off."

"I'm sorry to hear that," I said. It felt like the thing to say. "When?"

"Yesterday. After she talked with you. You two had a better conversation after ten years apart than we've had after being engaged for months."

I had nothing more to say. I still didn't get it. What could I have said? Finally, he moved on.

Sometimes you really have to wonder why things happen as they do. What had I done? A few years later I heard that he had been involved with young boys. I'm glad we met in the basement.

Fifteen years after that encounter in the basement our families had a barbeque at Claire's parent's place on the lake. I'd kept in touch with her brother, and his wife set it up.

I met and talked with Claire's husband. My wife talked with Claire in the kitchen. When my wife told Claire that I had always had a warm spot in my heart for her, Claire sagged over the counter and wept. I never knew. And then I wondered. I wondered about my prayer. I wondered about God's apparent answer. She never really stopped caring. Did I just misinterpret things?

If God knew, it felt like a dirty trick. Was that how Abraham felt?

It was only a trick if life is measured by accuracy. If it is measured by affection everything changes. When we are more concerned with the accuracy of language, we sometimes miss the warmth of the heart. Faith is not a matter of technique.

3...

The story seldom starts or ends with us. Abraham's father set out from Ur of the Chaldeans for Canaan.[24] He got halfway and stopped. Every sermon I have heard on the topic chastised either Terah or Abraham for stopping short. The Book doesn't say Terah was told to go to Canaan, and we are never told how the rest of Terah's life should have gone. Abraham was told to leave it all and go, but he apparently did not believe the adage that you can't take it with you. After his father died Abraham packed everything and moved on.

It's not that Abraham hadn't taken detours before the sacrifice of Isaac. The roads and rivers of God twist and turn their way through life. God said that he would make Abraham into a great nation beginning with the gift of a promised son. Sarah, his wife, was a beautiful but barren woman. Sarah wore the kind of attraction that men notice and Abraham knew others would willingly kill her husband to have her.

This happens even now. Many have stolen spouses away and left the abandoned partner crippled and gasping for breath. Abraham told Sarah to pose as his sister.[25] Other men took her, twice. It is too easy to think of Abraham with condescension, to consider his directions for his wife as cowardly, but there is a pragmatic temptation to preserve something, if not the best, when the threat is real.

I wondered in the first half of my life why Abraham didn't learn his lesson the first time? How could he be so stupid as to fail twice in the same way? I was ignorant of the wisdom that these problems are not rooted intellectually but emotionally. Was God taking time to teach Abraham not to fear? How many of us get that in one lesson?

---

[24] Genesis 11:31,32
[25] Genesis 12:11-13

I began violin lessons when I was five years old and continued for twelve years. I practiced five times a week. Life requires skill too. That takes practice and seldom comes in one lesson. The western world lives with the illusion that information alone transforms behavior. Just as my hands and arms learned musical techniques through practice, our minds and emotions need the repetition that creates wisdom and skill.

Why didn't I learn my lesson?

After my affair, after I left my wife for another woman, my former best friend said to me, "I get it that you had an affair. What I don't get is why you are going on with it."

Why do we go on with it? Why do we persevere in our failures and dysfunction? If we don't get it right, does the God who told Abraham to sacrifice his son really care about that? Maybe, but God did not keep bringing the circumstances around until Abraham got it right. What God did do was to intervene in anything that thwarted his purpose and blessing for Abraham and Sarah; even when they brought it on themselves.

The first time Abraham presented his wife as his sister the Lord inflicted serious diseases on Pharaoh and his household.[26] Pharaoh sent them packing (with the many gifts he had bestowed on Abraham). The second time Abraham let another man take his wife God talked to the ruler Abimelech in a dream.[27] All the women in Abimelech's realm had become barren. When Abimelech sent Sarah back, God told him Abraham would pray for the women and they would conceive

---

[26] Genesis 12:10-20
[27] Genesis 20:1-18

again. How does a childless man pray for fertility? Was God building Abraham's faith? What an unlikely way.

Ironically, when Abraham and Sarah were in Egypt and Abraham told Sarah to pose as his sister to save his own skin, God punished Pharaoh for taking Sarah, but he didn't even mention it to Abraham. Every sermon I have heard or preached talked about Abraham's lack of faith in those circumstances and the lessons to be learned. But there is no chastising, no rebuke or punishment for Abraham from God.

Time is relentless and there was still no child, no old age security, no joy, no future. Sarah had her own bout of pragmatism. She suggested her Egyptian handmaid Hagar have a child with Abraham.[28] Hagar conceived. Now, Sarah not only didn't have what she wanted, she had what she didn't want. Hagar despised her mistress. Sarah blamed Abraham and mistreated her handmaid. God blessed Hagar.

When Abraham was ninety-nine and Sarah was ninety God confirmed his covenant of blessing with Abraham.[29] Abraham prepared the ancient equivalent of contractual papers and God put Abraham into a deep, dark sleep and signed them himself. Do we ever become the friends of God without deep darkness? Before then Abraham and Sarah were called Abram and Sarai. When Abraham woke up God gave him and Sarah new names. They still meant the same thing, (the father and mother of many descendants) but their new names meant it even more. How often does a night of darkness make us more of who we are?

After all the detours (are they really detours?) and failures and grief and laughter the story still unfolded according to its purpose. In the end, none of the missteps

---

[28] Genesis 16:1-16
[29] Genesis 15

mattered. It didn't matter a bit that Terah didn't get all the way to Canaan. If it did, the Book doesn't make a point of it, doesn't say what might have, could have, should have been. It simply tells it like it was.

The pause in Haran, Sarah's time in other men's palaces; there may have been consequences but they didn't change the outcome. Abraham got to the Promised Land even if the only bit of the land Abraham would ever own was his wife's tomb. They had the promised son, the seed of a great nation, the son Abraham was ready to kill when God stopped him and told him he was a righteous man.

Abraham is an unlikely father of the faithful. But, that's what the book says he is. He is the biological ancestor of the Muslims and the Jews; he is the spiritual father of Christians too.

In a glass half-empty kind of way I learned about the stumbles of the saints as lessons to be avoided. *How could they...?* was the question that came up again and again as teachers told of Abraham's missteps. For a friend of God, Abraham got a lot wrong. There is something bigger than getting it all right. Could we tell our stories of faith and failure in a way that put us in God's good books instead of taking us out of the picture? In the irony of Abraham's faith an immoral act is why God credits him with righteousness. What does one do with that?

4...

At the last supper Jesus told the disciples one of them would betray him.[30] Peter said confidently that he wouldn't let

---

[30] Luke 22:21-34

Jesus down. Beware of unconditional promises of success or support. They are often the prelude to a failure.

"You'll deny three times that you know me,"[31] Jesus said. "Simon, Simon, [Peter's old name, not the new one] Satan has asked to sift all of you as wheat."[32]

Most lives get sifted. When it happens, spectators will focus on the impurities that are left behind. God is more interested in what is kept.

Jesus said more to Simon. "But I have prayed for you, Simon, that your faith will not fail."[33]

Isn't that odd? Why didn't Jesus pray that Peter wouldn't fail, that he wouldn't deny Jesus? That's what I would have prayed for, the ability to do the right thing. But God's one great thing is not the same as ours. God's one great thing for us is not that we always do the right thing, but that we trust him, even when we ourselves have been despicably untrustworthy.

Peter's faith in himself was about to take a beating. Jesus still believed in Peter, but not in the ordinary way. It's rare to find someone who believes in another without expecting anything for themselves. Jesus did not put his faith in people, but he had faith for people. The Bible says he did not entrust himself to people because he knew what was within them.[34] Was it because he didn't rely on others for his own hope that he could have such unconditional hope for them?

Before my eighth eye surgery I asked the anesthetist to put me out. I didn't want to go through it again. My left eye

---

[31] Luke 22:34
[32] Luke 22:31
[33] Luke 22:32
[34] Luke 2:24,25

was scarred and blurred. If the doctor could not repair the tear and detachment in my right eye I would be functionally blind.

"I can't put you under," the anesthetist said, "but I'll give you enough so that you're okay. And I'll be with you."

Once the intravenous needle was in my arm she held my hand as the drugs began to flow. When the needles injected around my right eye deadened the nerves it faded to black. After a few more minutes I felt a push on the outside edge of my eye socket.

"Keep pressure on this," the surgeon said to a nurse.

I felt no distress even though someone had just used a bar to pry my eye from its socket. *These are very good drugs,* I thought.

My inner eyes were gouged out too. That has made all the difference in my faith. After forty-five years of seeing things one way, I woke to find myself in a dark place. Rwanda. Abandonment. Divorce. I could no longer see things as I had. *I needed a change of vision.*

What transforms us from people of fear, pride and lust are not external observations, but a new way of seeing life. Our old feet will not take us there. Our old hands cannot embrace it. Our old eyes cannot see it. My loss of sight revealed what I was blind to.[35]

5...

I am trying to avoid saying that I believe God was in my moral failure, in my affair. There is a shadow where I believe it was his will; that when the Voice told me to *Go on* it was not simply an attempt to salvage a bad situation, but a

---

[35] John 9:39-41

path to the better, or even to the best. Not to being with a better person, but to becoming a better person.

I have heard the Voice for as long as I can remember. I could not say with certainty where it comes from. I believe it is divine, yet I accept that it is within me. It was the Voice that told me to prepare for funerals others had been asked to speak at. Yet just before those services I was called and asked to speak.

It was the Voice that told me to stand and speak at a conference where I was in the audience. Then I watched as God swept through that place and people stopped and wept and turned their lives. It was the Voice too that suggested I visit a particular antique store on my way to Whistler. I had a specific piece of furniture in mind; tall with doors and two drawers. They had nothing like that and when I was about to go the salesman called me back.

"Wait," he said, "We just had a container come in. Let's look." The piece I envisioned had just been unloaded.

The Voice guides me in my prayers, for I don't know what to say. It has prompted me to call others at just the right time. When I listen, the Voice speaks. I suspect the Voice is always whispering. Two days after my affair came out, when I asked what I should do, the Voice said *Go on*. I went home.

My goal as a husband had always been to make my wife, Mona, radiant, to make her the best she could be—as though any of us could own the responsibility or credit for that. I failed. Though I wanted to create freedom, wanted to build self-assurance, I didn't let her experience that for herself.

Conventionally, I was a good husband; always polite, persistently considerate. I wrote songs, bought gifts and held the door. I was friendly but not familiar with other women. In the end, convention isn't what matters most.

Seven years after our separation and divorce we were talking when Mona said, "You always said you wanted to make me the woman I was meant to be. Ironically, it was your leaving that accomplished it."

Oh the cost.

What if that is the goal? What if growth means more than being all right? What if faith means more than getting it right?

After a season of anger, years without a single Sunday when I went to church, I tried once more, and I went to my buddy's church. I sat in the back and cried softly as the Bible reader spoke:

> Therefore, as God's chosen people, holy and dearly loved, clothe yourselves with compassion, kindness, humility, gentleness and patience. Bear with each other and forgive one another if any of you has a grievance against someone. Forgive as the Lord forgave you. And over all these virtues put on love, which binds them all together in perfect unity.[36]

---

[36] Colossians 3:12-14 The other side of that coin is in the verses before.

> Put to death, therefore, whatever belongs to your earthly nature: sexual immorality, impurity, lust, evil desires and greed, which is idolatry. Because of these, the wrath of God is coming. You used to walk in these ways, in the life you once lived. But now you must also rid yourselves of all such things as these: anger, rage, malice, slander, and filthy language from your lips. Do not lie to each other, since you have taken off your old self with its practices and have put on the new self, which is being renewed in knowledge in the image of its Creator. (Colossians 3:5-10)

Compassion. Kindness. Humility. Gentleness. Patience. I am more of that. Not in spite of my moral failure, but because of it.

3. Even God Doesn't Love The Ones He Should

You don't have to be good to be loved. Neither do others.

Even God doesn't love the ones he should. We seldom do either. Love has never lived in the sphere of what one ought to do.

While some say passion and unlikely connections are an aberration of the weak, the love stories of the Bible are occasionally reliable, but almost never predictable. Abraham loves Sarah. Isaac loves Rebekah. Jacob loves Rachel. The patriarchs all found their loves at a distance from everything they knew, and loved at first sight. God loved Jacob even earlier.

Abraham's son Isaac married Rebekah but she was unable to conceive.[37] (How could they have known which of them was sterile? With men writing the story I wonder.) Once again, God brought the barren to life.

There was a lot of jostling in her belly and Rebekah asked, "Why is this happening to me?"[38]

How often does inner turmoil prepare us to listen? Of those who heard God in the Bible, how many were in crisis? God told Rebekah there were two nations in her womb. One would be stronger; the older would serve the younger.[39]

A board member once asked me to hold back on my strengths. I felt I had been restraining myself for years.

"Why don't you step up?" I asked.

But I did hold back. It was a mistake. We need to live up to our strengths. Servanthood and humility are not about

---
[37] Genesis 22:19ff
[38] Genesis 25:22
[39] Genesis 25:20-26

acting weak or dumbing down. Whether in families or organizations, acting weak doesn't serve anyone well.

When the twins were born to Rebekah the first was hairy and the second was grasping his heel as he came out of the womb. The oldest was named Esau. The younger was named Jacob; the name means heel grabber, deceiver, or supplanter.

Isaac and Rebekah's family, like every family in the Bible, was dysfunctional. Isaac loved the manly Esau more, and Rebekah loved stay-at-home Jacob. The babies grew up and Esau returned empty-handed from hunting one day. Jacob was stirring some stew and Esau pleaded for some.

"I'll sell you a bowl for your birthright to the biggest part of the inheritance,"[40] Jacob said.

Esau protested, but Jacob made him swear an oath, and the deal was done.

Years later, when their father Isaac was old and his eyes were no good, he called Esau to get some fresh game for him, cooked the way he liked.

"Get ready for my blessing,"[41] he said to Esau.

Rebekah heard it all and set a different plan in motion. She told *Jacob* to get two young goats and she cooked them just the way her husband liked. Then she sent Jacob in wearing Esau's clothes, with animal fur on his arms (to mimic the hairy Esau), and with the fresh cooked meat, just as their father Isaac liked.

Jacob came into his blind father's room and Isaac asked who was there. Jacob lied. Not just a little lie, but a masterful series of manipulations.

"I have done as you told me."[42]

---

[40] Genesis 25:27-34 author's paraphrase
[41] Genesis 27:2-4 a.p.

"How did you get the food so quickly?"[43] his father asked.

"The Lord your God gave me success,"[44] Jacob replied.

It is such an audacious lie that you expect God to strike Jacob down. But did He? Did God give Jacob success? If God didn't approve he never even whispered a word of rebuke. Before birth he chose Jacob over his brother.[45] Now, it was happening. Was it all in the plan? How else did I think Jacob would get the blessing? His father Isaac wouldn't have given it any other way.

Does God play by the same rules we're told he expects us to play by? Does God use immoral means for his ends? When God blessed Isaac, the Bible says God said it was because his father Abraham had obeyed God and kept all His requirements, commands, decrees and laws.[46]

At some point in my life as a minister I remembered that God did not issue any commands, decrees and laws for several hundred years after Abraham's death. In those days, I said that Abraham's faith made God look on him as though he had fulfilled all the rules. That may be true. But the attachment of blessing as a result of obedience sounds much more like the editorial addition of those in power in an attempt to keep followers under control. Nietzsche identified the principle. It happens in religious communities all over the world where position, possessions, and power provide all the wrong motives for spiritual leadership.

---

[42] Genesis 27:19
[43] Genesis 27:20 a.p.
[44] Genesis 27:20
[45] Genesis 25:23; Romans 9:10-13
[46] Genesis 26:3-5

After dinner and the blessing of Jacob, Esau showed up. His father shook like a leaf and told him the deal was already done. Jacob might have owned the birthright and the blessing, but he fled for his life before his brother the hunter could kill him.[47]

I assumed God's blessing meant life would get easier. For Jacob, God's blessing created animosity and conflict. Why? Years later, when Jacob's beloved son Joseph was enslaved in a foreign land, the book says he prospered.[48] The Lord was with him and gave him success in everything he did. Biblical prosperity has little to do with ease or comfort; it is not measured by what we have but by what we do with it. Prosperity is the ability to make more with what we have been given. If not a larger quantity, better still a greater quality.

On his flight away from everything he knew, Jacob fell asleep with a stone for a pillow.[49] I have slept with a stone for a pillow while backpacking in the wilderness. Stones make good pillows when you have nothing.

Jacob dreamed that night and saw a stairway resting on earth and touching heaven. Angels ascended and descended and God stood over the stairway. That night, God blessed Jacob with the same blessing he gave Abraham.

I will give you and yours this land.
You will have lots of descendants.
Everyone will be blessed through you and yours.
I am with you,
I will watch over you and bring you back,
and I won't leave you until I've done it all.[50]

---

[47] Genesis 27:41
[48] Genesis 39:1,2
[49] Genesis 28:10-15
[50] Genesis 28:13-15 a.p.

There are dreams more real than our waking moments. Jacob didn't say, "It was just a dream." It was the reality that shaped his life.

I had a strange dream. It was one of those dreams where you are sure you are not dreaming—it was that real. I drove down a country road in an old car like my parents had when I was little. A single barren tree was ahead in the field to the left. Someone was in the car with me and as I drove east and approached a T in the road, the man reached over with a knife and slit my throat from ear to ear. My head slumped on my right shoulder and as my blood drained I remember thinking, *Well, I guess that's it Lord, I'll be home shortly.*

Then I stepped on the gas hard thinking I would rid the world of the rotter who killed me. I was sure my dying was real. There was a dark pause, and then I was back at that T in the road. I had turned left. I could see a trail of blood where I had been killed and where the car had skidded off the road and into the tree. I had been brought back from the dead.

Though my dream was very different from Jacob's, the purpose was similar. Sometimes God prepares us for the future in our dreams. Not the dreams inspirational speakers encourage us to come up with on a scrap of paper, but the deep longings embedded in God's will and our own souls.

Nine months after my dream a man I worked closely with acted to end my ministry. I read the dream in my journal and realized it was all part of the plan. As I sit and write I run my fingers over the scar that stretches from one side of my neck to the other where my cancerous thyroid was removed. My neck has been cut from side to side and the life I had ended. I'm not what I was, but I am alive again and I have taken the road less travelled. I wonder, *What if it was God in the car with me?*

After the stairway to heaven Jacob travelled until he came to the land of the eastern peoples. There, at a well covered with a big stone Jacob saw Rachel approaching from the distance. There's no time better for falling in love than when we are alone and far from everything familiar. Shepherds were waiting there with their sheep and Jacob tried to persuade them to water their flocks and leave. The shepherds were waiting for help with the stone, but when Jacob saw Rachel close up, he rolled it away himself. There's strength in love.[51]

Four years after leaving my wife I was alone again when my buddy invited me to his fiftieth birthday party. Darla was there. In high school we were lab partners in biology and car-pooled from the outlying neighborhood where our minister fathers had bought or built homes. She was beautiful, smart, and fun. Her boyfriend was considered a lucky man. Darla and I dissected fetal pigs in class and studied together in her basement for an exam on human sexual anatomy and there was never an inappropriate word or touch. But we connected. Her boyfriend became her husband, but they arrived separately at the birthday party and spent no time beside each other that night. Darla paused as she was about to leave.

"I don't know if you knew; my husband and I are separated."

I was careful not to smile.

"Don't be a stranger," she said as she walked out the door.

Looking back I see the clear invitation, but I did not see myself that way in those days.

---

[51] Genesis 29:1-14

The next Saturday I thought of calling, but a man does not call on Saturday for a date. Even if it is for the following week, calling on a Saturday evening says either through a lack of attraction or planning, I am alone. The Voice in my head kept saying *call*. I argued, but at seven o'clock on a Saturday night I called.

I asked if she was free for coffee the next week.

"What are you doing tonight?" she asked.

"Nothing just yet," I said. "A glass of wine?"

"Have you eaten?" she said.

We met at a restaurant and immediately bumped into a former member of my church. I wasn't embarrassed any more. Four years after I failed my marriage three friends each asked separately on the same day whether I had forgiven myself. That was when the shame ended.

I couldn't give you a technique for ending shame. Most of the big transitions of my life have come as something of a surprise. I have been a planner, set goals and used a calendar to manage priorities, but those tools don't often work on the heart. When my three friends asked if I had forgiven myself, they created the emotional clarity that produced freedom.

It was easy to be with Darla. I wondered why she wasn't angry with me, but didn't ask. Her husband had had an affair and moved out.

After dinner she asked if I wanted to drive. We took her truck and wandered downtown and back through the suburbs. Where didn't matter, the journey was about the companionship, not the destination. One a.m., two a.m., three a.m. *The little hours,* as the Italians say to describe a late night.

"I told myself I would not date or see anyone for a year," Darla told me. She looked at her watch. "When you called yesterday..."

"Yes?" I said.

"It was a year to the day."

Darla invited me for lunch the next day, and I met her daughters. I liked them and they liked me, even with the wariness that children have for the first date after a parent has left, no matter how their parents have parted.

We chopped and stirred and simmered in the kitchen. Darla is a very good cook and bakes for fun. We talked about our pasts and our partners. You can't separate the person from their past experience and relationships. It is not a cause for jealousy when the new direction is good. Though her husband had moved out, they had not separated legally.

"Love is work," she said.

My former wife had said the same thing. I said nothing.

"Do you think love is work?" Darla asked.

"You cook a lot don't you?" I said. "Does it take a lot of work to create all the amazing dishes you do?"

"Sometimes it does."

"But does it feel like work?"

"No, I enjoy it."

"The work of love is mostly like that."

Jacob lived with Rachel's family and had worked with his uncle for a month when Laban asked Jacob to name his wages.

"I'll work seven years for your younger daughter Rachel," Jacob said. It seemed like no time at all because he loved her. Love lightens adversity.[52]

If love is a higher law, it doesn't mean the lower laws stop working. After seven years of work, Laban threw a wedding feast, but when Jacob woke up the next morning it was the homely older sister Leah in bed next to him! What went around when Jacob pretended to be his brother and deceived his father, came around on Jacob's wedding night when the less attractive sister pretended to be the one Jacob loved. I wonder how much he had to drink?

Love is never a commodity, but sometimes people's lives and bodies are treated as such. Perhaps Jacob offered seven years so Rachel would know how valuable she was to him. That wasn't the way she understood it. Some years later, when Jacob had two wives, two concubines, and several children, his first wife Leah offered her sister and Jacob's first love Rachel some mandrakes from the field in exchange for a night with Jacob.

"I have hired you," Leah told him when he got home, and so Jacob slept with her that night.[53]

When God told Jacob to leave his father-in-law and go home, his wives remembered that their father had sold them and they were happy to leave with everything that had once been his, including his gods.[54]

A few days later Laban realized his son-in-law, his daughters, grandchildren, and the flocks that had once been his were all gone. God told Laban not to say anything good or bad to Jacob. But it's hard to let others go.

---

[52] Genesis 29:14b-20 a.p.
[53] Genesis 30:14-16
[54] Genesis 31:14-19

"I could hurt you," Laban said to Jacob.[55]

We may want to hurt others when they have hurt us by leaving. Sometimes, if we can't get them to love us, we at least want to have some effect—pity, fear—anything to convince ourselves we're not insignificant.

I invited Darla to the symphony a week after our first date. Half an hour before I was to pick her up she called.

"My husband is here," she said. "I don't know why he came, but he's here."

"He heard I was taking you out," I said. They're not finished, I thought.

"Do you still want to go?" she asked.

"I'll be there in half an hour."

It was a beautiful evening and Darla was radiant. After the concert, and then drinks, we knew we had each other. My new apartment was blocks away.

"I'm going to step back," I said. "As much as I like you I don't think you're finished." Three weeks before I had wished I could redo the events that led to my affair, to taking another man's wife. This seemed like the time.

Darla's husband called the next day to tell me to back off and I told him the real issue was what he planned to do. I didn't talk to Darla again, but two years later I emailed hoping they had failed. She wrote back to say they were in a re-committed relationship. Still, I wonder. I had called one year to the day she and her husband had separated, the length of time she had decided would be right for her to see someone new.

---

[55] Genesis 31:29 a.p.

Have I been too noble in my ideas of love? What would Jacob have done? Would he have backed off from taking what he wanted because it didn't seem quite right?

Almost everything Jacob got, he took from someone else. He took his brother's birthright by capitalizing on a bowl of vegetarian stew. He deceived his father into giving him the blessing reserved for the eldest. God didn't punish Jacob, God took the things Jacob had taken from others and maximized the benefits. Jacob's crops grew a hundredfold. The sheep he took from his father-in-law reproduced in ways that multiplied Jacob's wealth and diminished Laban's.[56]

It sounds like a dangerous way to live, a recipe for gaining the world and losing one's soul. On the other hand, Jesus does tell the story of the master who took from an unproductive steward and gave it to a more profitable one. It's one thing to have God hand you something, it seems like something else to take it from another. Was that God's will for Jacob?

I am angry as I think about this. The idea of getting God's blessing by manipulating it away from others sounds like every narcissist I have met; those one-way streets who take and take without ever giving. I am poor and alone as I write this.

This unfairness is the fulcrum of our comfort and our frustration. It is infuriating to think that God loves the people who have manipulated and cheated us. It is comforting to know that God loves us even though we have been scheming and selfish. This is why it is impossible to know the forgiveness of God without forgiving others. *Forgive us our sins*

---

[56] Genesis 31:1-16

as we forgive those who sin against us. Grace is no theoretical exercise. I suppose the dark trio of narcissists, sociopaths and psychopaths live on some kind of fringe here, and though I don't believe they should be trusted, they can be forgiven.

Jacob took everything he could get. And God blessed it.

There are some things that love is not. Leah, the homely older sister, believed that if she gave her husband Jacob what he wanted he would be attached to her. After giving him three sons she thought she had it stitched up.[57] Love isn't like that.

Newton summed up much of life in his laws of force: For every action there is an equal and opposite reaction. Morality says the same thing: what you do determines what you get. Love is not like that. It is a difficult lesson to unlearn, especially for those who were raised to be good girls and boys. Men have more difficulty with this than women. There is a tendency to think that if we persist with attention, kindness, gifts and consideration, a person will eventually be attracted.

What are the unloved to do? When Leah had her fourth son, she didn't seem to care what Jacob thought. Instead, she praised God and named the boy Judah. He would become the black sheep of the family, the first man to truly extend grace, and the ancestor of the Messiah.

Leah saw the next two sons as gifts from God and said, "This time my husband will treat me with honor, because I have borne him six sons."[58] He didn't.

Therapists have talked to me about the healthy position of loving ourselves and not being drawn irrationally

---

[57] Genesis 29:34
[58] Genesis 30:20

to those who mirror our dysfunctions. This all makes sense, but it is an intellectual mansion while we live in the dog-house beside it.

When I started dating again after twenty-three years of marriage and another four with a lover, I discovered that while women are attracted to men who are good, a man who is all good, who is predictably good, is not as attractive. I have heard people (both men and women) share bad things they did. Usually, I liked them more after they told me what they had done. Don't ask me why, but when I told Mona I was leaving and she broke a wine glass over my head, grabbed a handful of hair and started punching, I admired her!

Years later I made a list, a full page of the qualities I was looking for in a woman. I met that woman and we dated several times. She was as smart as anyone I have met. Degrees in Zoology, Philosophy and a PhD in Experimental Medicine. She could quote Persian poetry and taught medicine. But we didn't quite click.

I suspect God can be like an Italian woman. If a man walks up to an Italian woman with any doubt he's done. She cocks an eyebrow, raises one side of her mouth in the same question she sees in the man: *Why would I like you?* But when a man walks up to women with confidence it is all different. She sees it and she likes it. Even if she doesn't let it show, even though she makes him persist—and women love persistence—she is drawn to that man. Then when she resists it is not to drive the man away, she does it because she wants to be pursued. Italian women have become this way as a defense against Italian men. While these women love confidence they despise cockiness and they have a nose as good as God's for arrogance.

On the night of a Christmas concert I stood in line for an hour beside two beautiful women on the one hundred and twenty-two steps to the Church of Santa Maria in Aracoeli. I said hello to one and asked a question. She answered as briefly as she could and turned away. I did not act rejected, I hummed and whistled and looked over at the other one and smiled and then ignored them for ten minutes.

"Where are you from?" the first woman asked.

"Vancouver."

"Have you heard of our Berlusconi? Our Prime Minister?"

"He's in a lot of trouble isn't he?" I said. He was on the front cover of a Canadian magazine for all his girlfriends and corruption.

"I love him!" the other woman said. "The press has made trouble for him. He has a sixty percent approval rating."

"What makes Italians love someone?" I said.

"Italians either love or hate," the first woman said.

I cocked an eyebrow and wondered.

"You have to be lucky," she said.

No one likes to think of love that way, especially God's love. But in the Bible God says "I love who I love and I hate who I hate."[59] That is what God is like! You need faith, not just in Him but in yourself! Faith that he's going to like you.

While unmet expectations may be the source of all conflict, people don't love us because we give them what they want, and we don't love others because they give us everything we want.

---

[59] Romans 9:10-13 a.p.

The fruit of Jacob's scheming did not fall far from the parental tree. Once his mother Rebekah had procured the firstborn's blessing for Jacob, she realized he might be killed before he could enjoy it. Rebekah talked to her husband Isaac about how she detested the foreign wives their other son Esau had married. Couldn't something me done for Jacob? So, Isaac sent Jacob away for something that seemed like a good reason.

The manipulative are good at getting others to do things for reasons they think are their own. My psychiatrist told me beauty ranks highest among the personal powers. I could not prove it statistically, except from my own life, but the beautiful often excel at manipulation. If there has been an early psychological wound, the likelihood is multiplied. The beautiful are not forced into the same molds of character as the rest of those who must live with the reliability of trust rather than immediate attraction. Once those being manipulated have nothing left to lose, they become either free or uncontrollable, depending on one's perspective.

Was Isaac still as attracted to Rebekah once he knew her well? Was she still beautiful to him? Was Rebekah's deception part of God's plan? Did she just live out what she heard God say when she inquired about the struggle within her womb before the twins were born and God said the older would serve the younger? How else would Jacob get the blessing? Rebekah didn't believe her husband Isaac would have given it any other way.

If we cannot secure love by giving others what they want, neither can it be taken.

Jacob had a daughter named Dinah and one day she went out to visit the women in the area. A man (Shechem, the favorite son of Hamor the ruler of that area), saw her and

54

raped her.⁶⁰ Jacob's sons were out in the fields so Jacob did nothing until they came back. When they did return they were furious.

This is the very strange part: The rapist's heart "…was drawn to Dinah daughter of Jacob; he loved the young woman and spoke tenderly to her. And Shechem said to his father Hamor, 'Get me this girl as my wife.'"⁶¹

Did he really think he could force a woman in the most intimate of encounters and then have her embrace him in the most intimate of relationships? No matter what your intentions, when you take what should only ever be given, something dies.

Shechem's father came to Jacob and asked for Dinah's marriage to his son. Dinah's brothers said that couldn't possibly happen with anyone who didn't share their covenant with God. The sign of their covenant was circumcision. The rapist went to the city gates, the place where business was done and convinced all the men in the area to be circumcised. The men saw it as an opportunity for prosperity. "If we intermarry, everything they have will become ours."⁶²

Three days later, while the men of that area were still in pain, two of Dinah's brothers entered the city with swords and killed every male. They took everyone and everything else as plunder.

About a third of the women I counseled as a minister were abused as children. Usually by someone close, someone they trusted. What have men been thinking? Is it any wonder that women are adamant in their demand for control over their own bodies?

---

⁶⁰ Genesis 34:1-31
⁶¹ Genesis 34:3,4
⁶² Genesis 34:21-23 a.p.

What is love? I find myself looking for a formula but there isn't one. Love isn't predictable, even for God. Pascal said "Love has its reasons that reason knows not of."[63] God, like us, embraces different lovers for contrasting reasons. Maybe God can even take hold of the parts that no one admires and embrace us. After the experiences of loving those I should not have, and lacking attraction for those who seemed well-suited for love, I concluded this was some flaw in me. But in God?

When Jacob camped while running away from his brother Esau, angels ascended and descended from heaven. When Jacob camped the night before his reunion with Esau, a relentless man fought with Jacob through the night. The same place that had been a stairway to heaven for Jacob became a wrestling ring.[64] When Jacob left home, the danger of his brother was behind him. On his return, the same danger was one day ahead. When he left he was encouraged by God. When he returned he was crippled. Both times he was blessed. Why?

The second time Jacob encountered God he thought he was lucky to be alive. "I saw God face to face, and yet my life was spared."[65] But, even though God himself said no one can see his face and live,[66] did anyone who saw God's face actually die? Abraham didn't die after God invited him to argue for mercy on Sodom and Gomorrah. Neither did Abraham and Sarah die when the Lord came to them in

---

[63] Pascal, Blaise, Pensees no. 680
[64] Genesis 28:1-19; 32:1-32
[65] Genesis 32:30
[66] Exodus 33:20

Sarah's old age with the birth announcement for Jacob. Samson's parents saw the face of God (twice) and didn't die when he brought another unlikely birth announcement and directions for the child. Moses, the one who was told no one could see God's face, conversed face to face so regularly that he glowed. Still, he wanted more.[67] It's true that Elijah was tucked in a crack of rock as God passed by. But what of Gideon, or Daniel and his three friends?

Apart from individual encounters, the Book says that God's face can be turned toward or away from people in blessing. Sometimes he turns his face in anger.[68]

Why did God wrestle with Jacob, especially when Jacob returned to a place that held such good history? Does every intimate relationship need a big fight? Can we ever know we are loved without conflict?

I never knew how to fight with those close to me. My former wife didn't either. I grew up with two parents who never argued in front of the children, with a father who told his children "Even when your mother is wrong, she is right." My wife's alcoholic father was sent packing when she was seven after the rest of the family came home and found him drunk out of his mind with a shotgun in his lap. For those who live in the extremes of all or nothing it's hard to know how to live with conflict. But it's hard to love without fighting.

I fought more with one beautiful lover than anyone I have known. She hated conflict too, but had better reasons for not wanting to fight. When she was a child her mother hid in the laundry basket to avoid beatings from the little girl's father. The mother blamed the little girl; her conception during an affair had cemented the marriage to a bad man.

---
[67] Exodus 33:18
[68] Isaiah 54:8; 57:17

Our fears provoked each other's anger. My jealousy, her elusive truth. My need to know, her need for independence.

"I always get my way," my lover said sadly.
"I'm tired of giving in," I said.

Jacob knew how to get his way. While most of us were taught to fall on our faces in reverent fear when God gives us a push, Jacob chose to fight. He would not submit.

On the journey home and on the eve of what could have been payback day from the brother Jacob cheated, God didn't descend on a glorious stairway from heaven. He showed up in the dark looking for a fight.

Those who wrestle with God may not win, but they don't lose. Job got his chance to argue with God and was overwhelmed—and comforted and blessed. At the end of the fight God broke open the strongest joint in Jacob's body; He dislocated Jacob's hip. Then God blessed Jacob again and Jacob limped on.[69]

Why does God hurt us, even cripple us? Why does he fight dirty? Why is it in our wounds that God blesses us? Why, when he equips us for one thing must he cripple us some other way? The fight was over; why cripple the man? It is hard to see the upside through our tears but there is a strength in the wounded that the relentlessly healthy never find.

The limp is real. One doesn't hear that much in sermons about encounters with God. Oh yes, "Meet God and he will break you…." But the limp is real. Jesus said if your right hand causes you to sin, cut it off. The loss is real. You

---

[69] Genesis 32:24-32

might stop sinning with that hand but there are a lot of other things you won't be doing either.

When the fight was over, Jacob had not won, he had simply not quit. He wouldn't let go. Even when the darkness was almost past, he wouldn't let go. Even after God had pulled him apart, Jacob would not let God go—and God tallied that as a win. God has a special place in his heart for those who never quit. He loves those who limp along. Especially those he crippled himself.

"What is your name?"[70] God asked at the end of the long night. "Who are you?"

"Jacob."

When we own our lives we are ready for change.

"Not anymore," God said. "Because you have struggled with God and with men and have overcome, your name will be Israel."[71]

From a name that meant Schemer (Jacob) to one that means Prince (Israel). Amazingly, God never mentioned Jacob's tenacious selfishness, or the cost to others. No lecture about selflessness or the need to serve others. God just really liked the fact that whatever Jacob was fighting for, he didn't quit. When was the last time I overcame God? After cancer, after losing my vocation and community, after divorce and going almost blind, after going broke, will God bless me because I am still hanging on? I would love to pin God to the mat, or at least keep him from leaving the ring with nothing to show for it.

When I had an affair I didn't just spend a night with a woman or take her body. I seduced her heart and took it from another. Is there a name for that? There is a painting by

---

[70] Genesis 32:27
[71] Genesis 32:28 a.p.

59

Rembrandt in the Louvre of *The Inspiration of Matthew*. A beautiful angel stands behind Matthew whispering into his ear. Is she inspiring or seducing him? Whether in pulpits or on the way to bed, the ability to change hearts is not so different. But for twenty-three years I never said an inappropriate word to a woman. I had a glass door on my office. I didn't go for coffee or lunch alone with a woman and wouldn't give a woman a ride in my car without calling my wife first. My old name could have been duty. What is my new name?

Israel asked God a question: "Please tell me your name."[72] God answered with another question: "Why do you ask my name?"[73]

There are several reasons for questions. Sometimes a person asks a question because they want the answer. Other times people ask a question because they want us to want the answer. When God asks a question the answer is really important. When God's question is left unanswered, it is an invitation.

"Why do you want to know my name?" God asks. *"Why do you want to know me?"* It is an invitation to intimacy.

If Jacob got a new name, did God get a new name too? Jacob's grandfather Abraham called God *the LORD*. Jacob's father Isaac called God *The Fear* after his father Abraham tried to sacrifice him. Before the fight, Jacob called God *The Lord your God* while deceiving his father, but now, now he calls God *El Elohe Israel*, *God, the God of Israel*. God's name is tied to Jacob/Israel more than any other individual in the Bible. *My God*; that's what Jacob calls Him. What is my own new name for God? *My Friend*.

---

[72] Genesis 32:29
[73] Genesis 32:29

In the morning, Jacob limped past the procession of those he had sent ahead to meet his brother Esau and his four hundred men. Instead of shielding himself behind those who had been arrayed from least important at the front to most important at the back, Jacob took his place in front of those who knew they were there to take the brunt of Esau's anger.[74]

Our wounds deliver us from at least two things: pride and fear. When our lives are torn apart we know we are no better than the least. The dysfunction that ranked relatives according to their favor and used them as shields was gone from Jacob. When we have fought with God we no longer fear men. After that kind of fight, even if we have been hurt, perhaps because we have been hurt, we no longer need to fear conflict with others.

I always thought Jacob hid behind them all, but in fact the story says that Jacob went to the front of them all. For years I misjudged Jacob. I saw Jacob, even after he had changed, through the lens of failure. I expected him to fail. After an affair, many people, even some of my own family, interpreted all my actions in the shadows of failure. A former friend called once to berate me. He assumed cheating sexually meant I was trying to cheat my wife financially too. We see the picture differently depending on what we use to frame events. Jacob expected his brother Esau to still see him as a cheat, to still be angry enough to kill him.

We're lucky if we get mostly free. Even after the reconciliation with his brother, Jacob went to live somewhere else instead of following Esau home as he said he would. They found themselves together again at their father's funeral just

---

[74] Genesis 32:7,8; 33:1-3

like Isaac and Ishmael did at the funeral of their father Abraham. Death separates some and unites others.

Why does one love another? God had a taste for Abel's offering, not Cain's. He tested Abraham, terrified Isaac. Loved Jacob, hated Esau. Anointed David, set aside Saul. Blessed Tamar, Rahab and Bathsheba. The Bible doesn't actually say that God loved Jacob more than Esau while telling the story of Jacob's life. It does say so in other places years later.

Who knows what God finds attractive? "*I love who I choose to.*"[75] That's love.

Stop trying to make sense of it all. Love more. Think about it less.

---

[75] Romans 9:13-18 a.p.

4. Integrity For Failures

Failure is not the end of goodness and integrity.
You don't have to be flawless to be good.

I needed a better question. For a lifetime I wondered how a very good man could do a really bad thing. There were the standard explanations. He didn't think about what he was doing. He wasn't very careful. He lacked self-control. He was never that good. Still, how could a good-hearted man like the Hebrew king David take another man's wife?

We all start somewhere.

David was a descendant of tragedy gone right. His great-grandmother Ruth was a foreign widow who lost her future before finding a fine man as she picked through the fields for food others had passed by.[76]

When David's predecessor King Saul stopped listening to God and started rationalizing his bad choices, God sent Samuel the prophet to tell Saul He had chosen another man for King.[77] Saul had disobeyed. He made excuses. He was afraid of what people thought. When Samuel delivered the news, Saul asked him to come and worship with him, to honor him before the people.

"God doesn't change his mind", Samuel said and refused to go. But that is exactly what God was doing; changing his mind. He regretted choosing Saul and chose David instead. Samuel changed his mind too and went with Saul to worship.[78]

---

[76] The Book of Ruth
[77] Prophets are the women and men whose mouths flow with God's words. They speak for God, and when they speak to God, we know they have been heard.
[78] 1 Samuel 15:10,11,23b-31

After that God sent the prophet Samuel to anoint David as the new king, but just because David had the anointing didn't mean he got the position right away. Years later Samuel died and David was still not king, but he was in King Saul's court.

One day while David played his harp to calm Saul's troubled mind, Saul hurled his spear at the young man. It's difficult to be comforted by someone we know will take our place. Saul knew what was coming, and that he had it coming. David ducked and fled.

While out hunting for David, Saul went into a cave to relieve himself while his men waited outside. David and his band were hiding deep inside.

"God has given him to you!"[79] David's men said, and David crept up behind Saul. But he only cut a corner from his robe. Afterward, David was conscience-stricken.[80]

"May the Lord judge between you and me," David yelled out to Saul from a safe distance. "But my hand will not touch you. From evildoers come evil deeds."[81]

David defined his life not in how others treated him, but in how he treated others. David even swore an oath not to harm Saul's offspring.

How do we let go of the expectation of good treatment? Not simply catching words of reproach, guilt and shame before they leave our lips, but living without the heart-dependence on fair treatment from others? Instead of eliminating our difficulties, how do we relinquish our reactions? This is not the same as commanding respect. (What an odd but accurate word to pair with respect: commanding.)

---

[79] 1 Samuel 24:4 author's paraphrase
[80] 1 Samuel 24:1-7
[81] 1 Samuel 24:12,13

There were at least three things that enabled David to hold his own good treatment lightly.

1. David knew who he wanted to be.

David knew who he wanted to be. My friend Anna told me that until we know who we are and what we want, it's hard to have a healthy relationship. Social scientists today speak of three centres of the self. Self-confidence, self-esteem, and self-concept.

Self-confidence comes from competence; our ability to do things well. When we create opportunities for success in the lives of our children and grandchildren we nurture this.

Self-esteem is our emotional opinion of ourselves. We feel better about ourselves when we make significant contributions (like our work), and engage meaningfully with other people.

Our *self-concept* is the collection of our thoughts about who and what we are. Self-concept is rooted in our values.

David grew in self-confidence as a young shepherd. His fight with the giant Goliath built even more confidence, but he had fought both a lion and a bear before he beat the giant.[82] When we remember battles we have won, it is easier to persevere and overcome new challenges and threats. David had self-esteem; his brother thought David was arrogant,[83] but he wasn't. Sometimes those closest to us will confuse confidence and arrogance. No one knows the heart but you and God. Given the choice, it is better to instill extra confidence into children. Life will inevitably chip away at it. It is harder to make a timid person bold.

---

[82] 1 Samuel 17:1-54
[83] 1 Samuel 17:28

David was able to be gracious because he had power. Grace and power belong together. Even if it is only for a moment, as when Saul went alone into a cave where David was hiding and David could have killed him but did not, it is when we have power that we can show grace. Even if it is only the power to choose our own response, to show others that they do not control our response, we can be gracious.

I learned two great lessons on grace from a bishop and a convict in Victor Hugo's *Les Miserables*. After being turned away everywhere, the convict Jean Valjean was welcomed for the night by the bishop. Only a day out of prison, and hardened rather than reformed by the experience, Valjean stole the bishop's silverware and fled. Valjean was captured and returned to the scene of the crime by the gendarmes.

The bishop, hearing Valjean's version of events—that he had given Valjean the silver—said, "But how is this? I gave you the candlesticks too, which are of silver like the rest, and for which you can certainly get two hundred francs. Why did you not carry them away with your forks and spoons?"[84] In that moment of grace Valjean was transformed. Instead of scrambling to meet his own needs, he used his strength to nurture and care for others.

The second incident is less quoted but shows another facet of grace with equal clarity. Years later, Valjean was a prosperous and kind man. While walking at night a thief accosted Valjean and demanded his money with the threat of violence. Valjean, his own strength considerable and undiminished, threw the thief to the ground and pinned him there with his knee upon the man's chest.

---

[84] Victor Hugo, Les Miserables, http://www.online-literature.com/victor_hugo/les_miserables/26/ September 6, 2012

Then Valjean took out his wallet. "What did you want of me? My purse? Here it is."[85]

Grace is never coerced and never so well-given as when both those giving and receiving know that the offender is at the mercy of the offended. That's where freedom is found. David had that kind of strength.

2. David believed God was the source of all justice.

The second thing that made David strong in the face of unfair treatment was his belief that God was the source of all justice. David would not kill Saul, even though he had several golden opportunities. Later, when David was king, he would not allow one of his men to harm an ignorant heckler who scorned and threw dirt on the king. Different religions hold a similar belief. Whether it is a sense of balance, karma or something else, it is the belief that there is a divine justice in the universe.

Like the rest of us, David's strength was his vulnerability too. For a man who killed lions, bears, and giants, David was very tolerant. He had little to fear and nothing to prove. It's not that David was never afraid. When he fled from Saul, David went to Achish king of Gath (one of the Philistine kings, of all people!). Sometimes the enemy of our enemy can seem like our friend. They are not the same. David realized where he was and feigned madness so his former enemies wouldn't kill him. Not everyone had forgotten his victory over Goliath and the subsequent Philistine rout. When we ourselves have felt our own weakness, or failed, we may hesitate to deal with the failures of others. Tolerance can be the motive for

---

[85] Victor Hugo, Les Miserables, http://www.gradesaver.com/les-miserables/e-text/section28/ April 21, 2013

grace, and it can be the root of discord when others see we are not dealing with things.

3. David believed in himself.

David believed in himself. He believed in his actions and he believed in his own heart. If we believe in ourselves we make mistakes, sometimes bad ones. If we don't believe in ourselves we won't do anything.

David and his band of men made sure that whenever they attacked a village and took the plunder, they left no one alive who could tell Achish.[86] How did I miss that for so many years? This man was ruthless. Why does the Bible mention David's affair as a failure but not the murder of entire towns? Why do I admire a man for not killing Saul, when he did kill women and children for supplies? Each life has its own bag of contradictions.

After a time, David returned home to Judah. In the custom of the day, David and his band of distressed, indebted and discontented men provided informal security for local shepherds and sheep and guarded them from bandits and marauders just one step below them on the social staircase. At sheep-shearing time, when the money came in, David, expecting some consideration, sent ten of his men to the wealthy Nabal whose flocks had benefitted from David's presence. Nabal was surly and mean and David's men went back with Nabal's message that David was a nobody.[87]

"It's been useless," David said. "All I've done hasn't helped me at all."[88]

---

[86] 1 Samuel 27:8-11
[87] 1 Samuel 25:2-11
[88] 1 Samuel 25:21 a.p.

Yeats said, "Too long a sacrifice can make a stone of the heart."

Despair is the threshold of disaster.

I remember the weekend I came to the same conclusion as David in my own life. For five months I had chewed on my rejection by the church in my final meeting with the board. I heard the nails banging into the lid of my vocational coffin when I was pushed to resign by friends I had stood with when death, disease and divorce had knocked on their doors. *This was planned*, I thought while I listened to explanations for each of my concerns. The chair asked if their responses addressed the issues I had raised.

"They are all good answers," I replied. "It's just that none of them are true."

No one blinked. How had they known my concerns? *I'm finished,* I thought.

Five months later I bumped into a former board member while out for a walk. She started to apologize and I interrupted with forgiveness.

"It was worse than you know," she said. It *had* all been planned.

"How did you know the questions I would ask?" I said.

"Your best friend told us," she said.

I had only told one person about my issues before the board meeting, and he wasn't just any friend. This was the friend I hiked into the mountains with to pray, and sat in silence with for hours at a time.

When I sat in my bed on the tenth floor of Vancouver General Hospital waiting for cancer surgery this was the friend who came to see me.

69

"Follow me," he said. "There's something I want to show you."

He led me down the hall and into a four-bed room looking up to the mountains on the North Shore.

Stopping at the first bed on the right he said, "This was my bed when I had cancer. God was right here with me when I had cancer and He's here with you too."

One dark night in India my friend and I walked to the train station in Bombay. Eyes from the shadows measured us and the size of our packs.

"Don't worry," my friend said, "I've got your back."

That was the friend who told my enemy of all my concerns. I wouldn't ask why until years later.

For months after I left the church friends avoided me. My well-intentioned wife stood at the door one evening, dressed and ready to go.

"Where are you going?" I asked.

She was going to a party at my best friend's home.

"They didn't invite you because they knew you wouldn't want to come," she said without a trace of guile as she walked out the door.

I really am all alone, I thought. There were other tragedies I will not speak of.

Meaningless, I thought after hearing of my betrayal. *None of the good I did has made any difference.* And then I thought... *Maybe if I do something bad that won't make any difference either.* I took my lover that Monday. That made a difference.

When we think the good we do is insignificant, we are at the door of dissolution and demoralization.

Nabal's marriage was one of those mysterious unions between a good woman and an awful man. Abigail was intelligent and beautiful, a wonderful combination! She heard of her husband's gall and told the servants to load meat and bread, cakes and wine onto donkeys. David was on his way with four hundred armed men to kill Nabal and every male in his household, but Abigail got to David first.

She took charge of the problem right away.

"My husband is a fool," she said. Then she appealed to David's own purpose and values. "God has great plans for you," she said. "Why taint them with revenge? May God hurl your enemies away like a stone from a sling."[89]

Brilliant! She even appealed to David's own history. That kind of social intelligence is a marvel in a good woman, and torture from a bad one. How could David help but fall in love with a woman like that?

A different sort of messenger came to me while I was sliding into the emotional part of the affair. A friend who had been part of the best small group Bible study of my life said he didn't know why, but he had a message for me.

"Don't give up and don't give in."

The words resonated but I discredited the man. A week before another friend from the same Bible study told me he had hit on her. Perhaps that was why he knew what to say to me.

It didn't stop me from talking with another woman. My prayers didn't stop me. In the past I had been held back from sin like a car riding the guardrail while rounding a treacherous curve. This time there was nothing holding me back. I never stopped myself. I gave myself. In an irony that rocked my world, I opened myself more fully than I ever had

---

[89] 1 Samuel 25:23-31 a.p.

and the intimacy astounded me. The intimacy was immoral and inconsiderate; it was a blissful enlightenment.

When a person feels bad enough for long enough, they will find a way to feel better. For some it is drugs or alcohol, for others it can be work or gambling. In my desert of loneliness it was intimacy.

After a few months of the affair being public a man called to list my sins.

"I bet you don't even enjoy the sex because of your guilt," he said.

Sometimes we enjoy sex more because it is forbidden.

I wrote and apologized for my affair to a long time friend who had asked me to speak at an event she organized. She replied and wondered if my recent failure was the way I had always been. A friend of my wife's wrote to say that my heart felt nothing for my wife. I had knelt in the bathtub and watched my tears flow down the drain. Whatever others had done to me, what I did to my wife was worse. Commitment is a funny thing. One facet looks like duty. Another is all about attraction. The former seldom stays fresh without the latter.

How could a good man break completely down, abandon his morals and deeply wound those closest to him? Moral failure is seldom explained even when it is described.

In the spring, when kings went to war, David didn't.[90] I have wondered why. Was it his own kind of mid-life crisis? Like any good story, David's doesn't give us many details on motive so we can find our own way in. Was he wondering if the annual ritual of conflict was meaningless in the same way most of us do about our own vocations?

---

[90] 2 Samuel 11:1

At the end of the day as David walked on the roof-top of his palace he saw a beautiful woman bathing.[91] He inquired. She was the wife of one of David's best soldiers. Uriah was out fighting while the king stayed home. David sent for Uriah's wife, slept with her, and she went home.

Later she sent a message. "I am pregnant."[92] (Why is it that woman after woman cannot conceive in the Bible, yet when David and Bathsheba sleep together just after her period she gets pregnant right away?)

There is something especially devastating about sinning with our eyes open.

After a clean break-up with Mira the door opened once more and she invited me to come over for the night. I said no, but later as I lay awake and alone in the reclining chair I slept in while my torn retina healed, I asked myself *Why?*

I got up to go to her and the Voice said *If you go to her now you will do real damage to yourself.* I drove over, tapped on her bedroom window and she took me in. I was a sincere man before then.

Willful sin lives in a category of its own. Dante said the shallowest level of hell was reserved for lovers who were immoral but sincere. Once our eyes are opened, not just intellectually, but emotionally, we sell ourselves into slavery with just one more step; we receive less and less while more and more is demanded.

When Bathsheba sent the message that she was expecting, David sent for Bathsheba's husband on the pretext of asking how the battle was going.[93] Then David sent him

---

[91] 2 Samuel 11:2-5
[92] 2 Samuel 11:5
[93] 2 Samuel 11:6-13

73

home to be with his wife. But Uriah didn't go. He slept on the ground outside the palace.

"How could I eat and drink and make love to my wife while my comrades are facing peril?"[94]

Good question. How did David? How did I choose pleasure when my family and friends were in crisis?

I went away for a road trip on my Honda VFR750 motorcycle. After two hours of freeway I was beyond Hope, the small town two hours East of Vancouver. Highway 1 curved through the Fraser Canyon, boring through tunnels and tracing mountainsides until the dry heat of the interior of British Columbia. I rolled toward my childhood home, Kelowna. A day later I headed south along Okanagan Lake and then west for the return to Hope.

On the steep grades of Highway 3 there are runaway lanes that cut away from the pavement and slash through the trees in a sharp arc up the side of the mountain. They are refuges for big trucks whose brakes have gotten so hot from the ongoing strain that they have given out. There are signs of their approach.

Six hundred meters to runaway lane.
Three hundred meters to runaway lane.
One hundred meters to runaway lane.

As a child I imagined white-knuckled truckers listening to their diesels scream and hoping they could stay on the road until the way of escape. After each missed opportunity it would be harder to stop. At the bottom of those hills are sharp hairpins, sometimes over bridges that traverse deep ravines. You wouldn't make it around those corners without brakes.

---

[94] 2 Samuel 11:11 a.p.

When I was young, my parents, two sisters, baby brother and I came down one of those hills and saw skidmarks slewing to where a blackened tanker truck traversed most of the roadway. The trailer brakes had seized and set the truck across the road. A station wagon with a family inside had not been able to stop and had wedged itself beneath the tank before some spark ignited an inferno. Charred steel and melted asphalt were all that remained. The family was covered with a tarp.

There are casualties when you can't stop.

There were opportunities to stop the affair before it became intimate. For twenty-three years of marriage I had bolted and barred the doors of my life. Temptation came through a window I overlooked. After leaving the church in the biggest rejection of my life it seemed so unlikely that any woman would be attracted to me. Insecurity masqueraded as safety. Once my carefully constructed boundaries were breached, I didn't have the strength to fight.

David didn't stop when he saw Bathsheba. He didn't stop when he found out she was pregnant. He still didn't stop when her husband came home from the battlefield but would not sleep with her. David sent Bathsheba's husband Uriah back to the battlefront with a letter for the general.

"Put Uriah out in front where the fighting is fiercest. Then withdraw from him so he will be struck down and die."[95]

How does a man who has been so relentlessly good go as far as that? How does a man who fought lions and bears and giants, a man who spared his foes and pledged his protection for his enemy's family fail like this? He had been

---
[95] 2 Samuel 11:15

ruthless in the past, but then it was against his enemies and to save his own life. Now he was ruthless with the life of a man devoted to him. Had David reached the point that many leaders come to, when looking good means more than being good?

When we have stood up front, learned to live with earned trust, it is hard to let that go. Why wasn't David at the battlefield? That man loved to fight. Was he living in that season when we realize nothing ever changes just as we are about to? Had life lost its challenge? I don't know. But the clues from David's life help us discover our own motives.

We bring the same strengths to our failures that we bring to our successes. A persistent man brings determination to his failures as well as his successes. A patient woman will wait for one thing as well as another. A creative person may be even more ingenious in their immorality than in their ethics. The great fail on a larger scale.

Eventually, it is out of our hands.

After the affair was public, in the days when old acquaintances and former parishioners saw me from the far end of grocery aisles and walked away, a young man from the church invited me to coffee.

"It was inevitable," he said.

"How do you figure that?" I asked.

"With every success people trusted and expected more of you. You had to fail eventually."

He had known his own tragedy when his father couldn't cover any more expectations and took his own life. The young man was as bravely honest with his own hopes as anyone I know and he settled into a good life. When we own the mess, we're ready to move ahead again.

When Uriah's wife heard that her husband was dead, she mourned for him. After the time of mourning was over, David had her brought to his house, and she became his wife and bore him a son. But the thing David had done displeased the LORD.[96]

That is a frightening thought.
God sent the prophet Nathan to David with a message and Nathan wrapped it in a story.

There were two men in a certain town, one rich and the other poor. The rich man had a very large number of sheep and cattle, but the poor man had nothing except one little ewe lamb he had bought. He raised it, and it grew up with him and his children. It shared his food, drank from his cup and even slept in his arms. It was like a daughter to him.
Now a traveler came to the rich man, but the rich man refrained from taking one of his own sheep or cattle to prepare a meal for the traveler who had come to him. Instead, he took the ewe lamb that belonged to the poor man and prepared it for the one who had come to him.[97]

David was furious with what he heard, mad enough to have the selfish man killed. David felt the injustice before he knew it applied to him.

---

[96] 2 Samuel 11:26,27
[97] 2 Samuel 12:1-4

"You're the man,"[98] Nathan said.

In that blaze of enlightenment, David humbled himself. "I have sinned against the Lord,"[99] David said.

I am the man.

There were consequences. I thought I had lost everything, but I lost more; lost more friends, more of my reputation, more money, more of my health. The child of David and Bathsheba's love died. Why the baby? Why did God take the baby? Why does God punish the innocent for the sins of the guilty?

One could argue that it was to create a change of heart but David had already repented when God took the baby.[100] Maybe it was for everyone else, for all those who live by the rule of consequences instead of from the heart. If those people thought there were no consequences can you imagine what would happen? It's harsh, but it could almost be.

Carl Jung, the nineteenth century psychoanalyst contemplated the nature of a created world in which moral failure (or sin) was not only a possibility, but a certainty in God's mind. Jung concluded that God, who knew everything and could do anything, thought a world in which people failed was better than a world in which they did not.

The Bible itself says that God chose a path of redemption, or re-creation, before the beginning of the world.[101] Humanity's failure was never a surprise to the divine. After Jung struggled and failed to resist his own unforgivable thought as a young man, Jung concluded that a world with

---

[98] 2 Samuel 12:7
[99] 2 Samuel 12:13
[100] 2 Samuel 12:13-18
[101] Ephesians 1:3-10

grace is better than a world without failure.[102] There is a depth and sweetness to life after failure that is not found without it.

After praying, after the child died, David got up and went on.[103] How does one do that?

I have heard preachers I respect say that David's life was never the same after his adultery. That's true. His own son Absalom plotted against him and even overthrew his father before David's soldiers conquered and killed Absalom.

Before that ever happened though, Absalom's sister Tamar was raped.[104] David was furious, but did nothing about it. Absalom was furious too. After waiting two years he took matters into his own hands, invited his sister's rapist to a party and killed him there.[105]

Absalom fled for his life believing his father would be angry. For three years David grieved and missed his son Absalom, but he neither saw him nor sent for him. David's friend devised a plan for reconciliation and David had Absalom returned to the city, but for two years he would not see him. When Absalom's first daughter was born, Absalom named her after his sister Tamar.

In time, Absalom caught the attention of those who felt they could not get the king's ear. Absalom felt the same way. With a few choice words to those looking for justice ("I would give you what you want."[106]—how often is deceit in that promise?) Absalom overthrew his father the king and David fled from the city.

---

[102] C.G. Jung, Memories, Dreams Reflections, Vintage Books, pp. 39ff
[103] 2 Samuel 12:18-23
[104] 2 Samuel 13:1-21
[105] Samuel 13:23-29
[106] 2 Samuel 15:4-6 a.p.

How different would things have been if David had stepped in when his daughter was raped? In the end, when his few loyal troops overcame Absalom and killed him, David would rather have wept for Absalom than thank his true friends.[107] Was the man who had seduced someone else's wife remembering his own flaws when it came time to do something about someone else's failure? Was it David's own sense of guilt, or the perceived need to be hard on failure, that kept him from embracing Absalom even when he came home two years before his revolt? Was it unavoidable because God said, "Out of your own household I am going to bring calamity on you."?[108]

Just because we've failed doesn't mean we can't say someone is wrong. There is a time to lose our arrogance but not our authority. David's family needed him to speak up.

David knew that God, like women, is better approached with the language of the heart than with a to-do list. He wrote a poem. In the fifty-first Psalm David owns his life, he shows a little faith, and he offers to help others. David doesn't just ask God to blot out what was wrong. He asks for restoration of all that is right: purity, steadfastness, joy, and willingness.

People don't get better because they feel persistently bad. We make lasting change when we feel better because of it. It is all tied to God's presence for David.

In my own dissolution I looked for leaders who could guide me. Religious leaders and educators who had been close either threw up their hands or didn't return my calls and letters. I went through four therapists, and found a few friends who would not tell me what to do, but who stuck with me and

---

[107] 2 Samuel 17:24-18:33
[108] 2 Samuel 12:11

listened persistently. How many people have looked for help and insight not just into how to be good, but into how to live when we are *not* good? What price was it worth to have a guide through failure like the fifty-first Psalm?

In his Inferno, Dante guided me through my own emotional hell. At one point the disembodied shadows wondered why Dante's body cast a shadow in hell. His good guide Virgil says:

> Death does not have him yet, he is not here
> to suffer for his guilt…
> …but that he may have full experience.[109]

I am grateful for the failures of good men who show me the way. After failure, after the emptiness, there is a hunger for life, questions endure. *How can I be healed? How does one create life from stone?*

A year and a half after I finally left Mira the sculptors of Italy showed me how. I had done what I could to close out the difficult decade of my forties. I left for Italy.

Inside the Galleria Borghese, the first two rooms were filled with more sculpture than any museum in my home city would see in a lifetime. In the third room, my attention was arrested.

The sculpted David posed with his sling about to let fly. The unseen giant Goliath would catch the stone between his eyes and the sculptor Bernini captured the anticipation. It is a moment of transcendent wonder. David's torso is twisted with the strength that brings power when our core is involved. The muscles are torqued in a way one knows is true, but it is

---

[109] The Portable Dante, Mark Musa ed., Penguin Classics 1995, Inferno Canto XXVIII, verse 48, p.153

the face that says everything about the strength of this man. David's young forehead is creased and his brows focus down and in. His jaw is not slack, but—and this one detail tells all—David is biting his lip! In Bernini's display of the encounter between good and evil, a story of divine empowering, we recognize how very human the chosen are. They bite their lips.

With that image David became real to me. Whenever I have shot a basketball, hit a baseball or wrestled, I have bitten my lip in the moment when energy and attention converge. With that one image Bernini touched my soul. It is so easy to distance ourselves from the saints; to think they are of a different fibre than us. We capitalize on the lessons, encouragement, comfort and correction of these stories when we realize the people of the bible were women and men just like us. They were liars, cheats, adulterers and murderers and God loved them. If that was true for them, it can be true for me!

We begin the journey of restoration by being real. There was a point in my immorality when I could not change, but I chose to be real. No more lying to my wife or to my mistress. For the few who came close enough to hear, I was honest. It was the first step of humility and integrity. Authenticity is at the root of integrity.

Just a few steps away from Bernini's David in the Galleria Borghese is Caravaggio's painting of David holding the severed head of Goliath in his left hand and the giant's sword in the right. Caravaggio's paintings are dramatic, but no more so than his life. He drank heavily and fought often. In one brawl he killed a man and fled from Rome with a price on his head. On his way back to Rome in hope of a pardon Caravaggio painted *David with the Head of Goliath* and sent it ahead. The young David may be an early version of

Caravaggio. The face of Goliath with his downcast eyes is Caravaggio's self-portrait. The inscription on the blade of the sword is an abbreviation of the Latin phrase *Humilitas occidit superbiam*. Humility kills pride.

The humility of the biblical David might not have come when we think it should have, but it came when the prophet Nathan confronted him, and it never really left David again. That kind of humility, the kind that relinquishes pride, fear and control, the kind that accepts who we really are and takes responsibility for what we've done, that kind of humility seldom comes through anything but actual failure. Humility is not an idea.

God heard David's prayer and ultimately spoke of him as a man of integrity;[110] a man with a heart like his own. How does God do that? *How does God restore a life?*

For many years I believed integrity was the unflawed quality of things that had never been broken, the character of people who did not fail.

We get the word integrity from the Latin *integritas*; something of unimpaired condition, complete and sound, pure or chaste, honest and innocent. No surprise there. It is an attractive picture of goodness. For years I lived with the conviction that integrity was all of these things. And, without ever thinking or saying it explicitly, I believed integrity meant a life without failure. I was not alone in that belief.

The verb forms of *integritas* tell a different story. *Integratio* speaks of renewal and restoration. *Integro* means to make whole, restore or repair; to renew, repeat or to begin again. In Latin, it seems, there is nothing of integrity that has

---

[110] 1 Kings 9:4

not been fixed. Integrity doesn't mean we've never failed, it means we've been repaired, we've begun again.

In other ancient languages like Hebrew and Greek, there was no exact word for integrity. Someone was said to be a person of integrity if they were a *true* person, someone firm and reliable. Beyond that, a true person is forthright about both the good and the bad.

No one gets it all right. Disappointment, weakness or disaster can bring dis-integration. People come apart, but they can be put back together.

The test of integrity is not in the past but the present. Something that has been unreliable in the past may have been repaired and trustworthy now. Something that has been reliable in the past may be fatigued or damaged and about to fail. How are we to know?

There are signs of imminent failure, even in someone with a pristine record. Deep weariness, a change in personality, depression, or pride can all come before failure. The discerning will step in or step out before a fall. Integrity is not simply a condition, it is a process.

There is an old Greek word, *katartizein*, that parallels the Latin verbs *integratia* and *integro*. In medicine the word is used for setting a broken limb or for putting a joint back into its place. In politics it is used for bringing together opposing factions so that the government can go on. In the Bible it is used to describe mending nets, and the Apostle Paul used the word in a couple of letters to describe the training and discipline of people for service and after a failure. That kind of discipline wasn't about kicking someone out, it was about putting them back together.

The defining question is: *What does this person need to put it together?*

I went to the Galleria dell'Accademia in Florence to see Michelangelo's *David*. Once through the gift shop and past the desk for audio-guides you go through a door and turn right into a long hallway. On either side were four partial figures still trapped in the stone as well as their chains. They are *The Four Prisoners*. At the end of the hallway, under a dome specially built for him, was David.

Michelangelo's *David* is a giant. He is fourteen feet tall and from his pedestal he dominates everything around him. From the front he seems almost serene. His body is perfectly muscled but not tense. After a few minutes I walked to the right, to where David is looking. Things changed.

The toes on David's left foot are gripping the earth. He's getting ready to let it go. His brow is furrowed and his face is fixed in a gaze that is intense and aggressive without any bit of fear. His eyes look past you to what is beyond and bigger. His left hand holds the end of the sling. His right hand holds the stones. He's not clenching them, he's holding them like someone sussing the weight of something. The hands are monstrous, out of all proportion really. It may have to do with perspective, where Michelangelo thought we would be looking from, or it may be that Michelangelo is saying that one day long ago David *was* the hands of God.

I think Michelangelo was the hands of God for the years of his life. Though dissection of human bodies was both immoral and illegal in his day, young Michelangelo once made a crucifix for the Church of Santo Spirito in Florence out of appreciation for the prior who left some rooms for Michelangelo where he often flayed dead bodies to discover what was beneath. The real stuff of beauty goes all the way to the core.

When Michelangelo finished sculpting David, the Gonfaloniere of Florence looked up and said the nose seemed a bit big. Michelangelo gathered his hammer and chisel and bits of marble from the scaffolding as he climbed. He had already taken away everything that was not part of the statue, but, after clinking and clanking and letting bits of marble slip from his fingers while blocking the view, he pronounced the work finished.

"Now you've really brought it life," the critic said.

Michelangelo had in fact brought it to life. The marble had twice been rejected by other artists as brittle and unusable. One had begun and left a hole through the stone where the legs would be. No one else would touch it.

But, as Michelangelo's contemporary and biographer, Vasari, said, "Michelangelo worked a miracle in restoring to life something that had been left for dead."[111]

Restoration is not just about fixing the flaws. It is about finding the glory. Michelangelo found the glory in a block of marble. The goal was not a deadline. God foresaw glory in the life of David. The next child David had with Bathsheba became a wise king and the ancestor of the Christ.

Too often people told me God would redeem something from the ruins of my life. God does more than that. In the transformation of hearts from stone to flesh, failure is often as important to the process as repentance.

This whole business is usually a surprise. David didn't start putting his life right because he read a book or thought through the priorities of his life. God surprised him. That's God's way.

---

[111] Vasari, The Lives of the Artists, p.328, Penguin Classics

As I waited for the last high speed train of the night from Florence to Rome I realized my life was being restored. God is a master of creation and restoration. Sometimes he works directly, other times he uses the hands of others to bring to life that which had been left for dead. Those close to me, near enough to get their hands on me, didn't tell me what to do. For years they listened and waited for me to come to myself.

I used to question how David could have failed so badly. Now I know no one gets it all right and I wonder why a good-looking, sensitive, musical, passionate, rich and powerful man wasn't seducing women and killing opponents all the time. But that is not my better question.

After telling my wife there was no hope for us and driving away, I wept until I had to pull to the side of the road. I called the nearest real friend, a wise and good-hearted man who had been my college president and later came to work with me.

"What is wrong with me?" I asked through my sobs.

"Maybe you need to ask what is right with you," he said.

5. Post-Moral Man

Obligation doesn't empower goodness, inspiration does.

The Problem

Just because you should doesn't mean you can.

There was a war going on inside the Apostle Paul when he wrote *"The things I know I shouldn't do are the very things I find myself doing; and I'm unable to do the good things I want to."*[112] The man who had been flawless at keeping the Jewish religious law, who had a dramatic conversion complete with voices from heaven, and who wrote one third of the New Testament, found himself unable to do the right thing.

Just because you don't want to doesn't mean you won't.

Saul, (the name he went by before God gave him the new name Paul) was on his way to Damascus to persecute Christians when he was knocked from his donkey and struck blind. There are things you won't see until you've been blinded. For three days Saul couldn't see anything.[113]

I was practically blind for considerably longer. Three years after leaving the church, two years after I left my wife, and after a series of operations on my left eye that left it scarred and my vision blurry, my good right eye went bad.

"It's a major tear and it will take a significant operation to fix it," Dr. Shepherd said.

"Will I be blind?"

---

[112] Romans 7:15, 19 author's paraphrase
[113] Acts 9:1-9

Strands of blood floated in the jaundiced fluid of my right eye. I couldn't help myself, I cried.

"Will I need to find a new way to live?" I asked.

"You won't see from that eye for a while. It could be dark for up to a month and then the vision from the two eyes probably won't align for a while."

Post-surgery I went home to the same recliner I had rested in after the last seven operations. Sitting at forty-five degrees kept the injected gas bubble floating up against the torn pieces inside my eye. Dark room. Dark eye. Dark time.

I felt my way along the wall to the bathroom. Like a man almost submerged, a slim crescent of sight bobbed on the top of my vision. The orb of vision grew with time. After a month the right eye was clearer, but when I looked at things the image in my repaired eye was down a foot and over to the right. It was confusing, nauseating.

"Will it get better?" I asked the doctor.

"It can take time," he said. "Sometimes it's more than the mind can compensate for."

Sometimes we see more than our mind and emotions can consolidate. Two years before leaving the church I was invited on a mission of peace and reconciliation to Rwanda; it was the seventh anniversary of the genocide. I saw bullet holes in every building. Blood stained the walls of churches and bones filled concrete crypts that lined the earth like scars. The killers had waited for people to congregate in places of sanctuary. In a church in Ntarama, a small village in the middle of nowhere, the bodies are still draped over the pews as a witness. The smell was strong. Five thousand skulls were stacked in sheds to the side of the church. The smallest were in the front, some cleft in two.

Rwanda was described as the most Christian nation in Africa. How does one put that together?

Six weeks after my eye surgery I woke up seeing one thing instead of two. The mind does that, it pulls things together and uses what is clear. Later in the day, when I was tired, my mind couldn't hold the two together any longer. Life's like that.

After three days of darkness God told the prophet Ananias to go and heal Saul's eyes.[114] Ananias didn't want to go. He had heard of Saul's reputation as a zealous persecutor of Christians. Saul held people's coats while they stoned the disciple Stephen to death. Still, Ananias went, laid hands on the man, called him *Brother Saul*, and "something like scales fell from Saul's eyes."[115]

Once Saul's sight was restored he disappeared for years. The old crowd had no use for him. The new crowd didn't trust him. He was a voice without an audience. An encouraging man had to go and get him before he began talking again. They say God doesn't waste the talents of a person's life, but He often lets them ferment.

My friend Martin invited me to preach at his church a year after Mira and I broke up. My life was still messy. Martin had listened for years as I cursed others and wept for my own failures. In those days Martin waited on the phone while I lay on the floor unable to speak and my tears soaked into the carpet. My tears did not change me. We seldom sustain a good direction because we feel bad.

---

[114] Acts 9:10-19
[115] Acts 9:18

I spoke at Martin's church about guarding the heart; for the heart is the wellspring of life. Before, I had preached with the credentials of a good life.

"Today I am preaching because of my failures," I told the congregation.

How does one restore the heart?

The Cure – death to the moral obligation of the law

Knowing the rules doesn't enable us to keep them. We don't go the right way because we know we have gone wrong.

Shortly after the birth of my first child I bought a car. It had a reputation for reliability and seemed to be in great shape. I was driving through the parking lot at the bank when the car shuddered and quit. I turned the key and it ran for a moment before quitting again. The fuel gauge said there was some gas left. I turned the key again and again. Each turn produced a false start. I looked under the hood and could see no problem. I called the dealership where I bought the car and described the symptoms to a mechanic.

"It sounds like it's out of gas," the man said.

"But the gauge says there's still a bit in the tank."

"The fuel gauge doesn't put gas in the engine," the mechanic said, "it just measures what's there. Put more in and try it again."

It worked.

The law is like that; it measures, it doesn't empower. The law can prescribe what we should do and condemn us when we don't, but it can't enable us to fulfill its requirements. It stands outside rather than moving us from within. God never meant the law to fuel good behavior. He meant it to show us our need of Him.

I would not have known what sin was had it not been for the law. For I would not have known what coveting really was if the law had not said, 'You shall not covet.' But sin, seizing the opportunity afforded by the commandment, produced in me every kind of coveting. ...I found that the very commandment that was intended to bring life actually brought death... Did that which is good, then, become death to me? By no means! Nevertheless, in order that sin might be recognized as sin, it used what is good to bring about my death, so that through the commandment sin might become utterly sinful.[116]

The law of God, the holy, righteous, good law of God doesn't make us good, it shows us that we are not.

"What a wretched man I am! Who will rescue me...?"[117] the Apostle Paul said.

That man was in a moral crisis. Paul described the fruit of flesh without Spirit: "sexual immorality, impurity and debauchery; idolatry and witchcraft; hatred, discord, jealousy, fits of rage, selfish ambition, dissensions, factions and envy; drunkenness, orgies, and the like."[118]

Without saying what his particular problem was, Paul couldn't do what he should. He couldn't stop himself from what he should not do. For those accustomed to success that's especially devastating. I had been taught the verse about wretchedness and rescue theologically, but the real lesson is

---

[116] Romans 7:7,8,10,13
[117] Romans 7:24
[118] Galatians 5:19-21

emotional and relational. By saying our moral crisis is emotional I do not mean it is thoughtless or irrational. There are times we feel or behave badly because our thinking is wrong. We can be transformed through the renewing of our minds; but that is often an alignment of insight and emotion. The question of deliverance is not theoretical when we are desperate but powerless.

A chapter before Paul's season of powerlessness, he told the Christians in Rome to reckon themselves dead to sin. That's when he found out he wasn't. Transformation often begins with the recognition of what we are not. I am learning what I am not. I am not as good or as strong as I once thought.

After I told Mona of the affair we went to a counselor weekly. It wasn't working.

"What about your vows? What about your duty?" Mona asked.

I couldn't answer. After living a lifetime from those values, I was out of fuel.

"Can't you see?" the counselor said. "If he's going to come back, it will need to be from something more than that. Greg's not living on that page anymore."

Morality died a messy death in my life. Paul's cure for moral failure was death—death to the law. When we cannot fulfill our obligations, cannot live up to what is expected, the first step is death. No one expects anything from a dead man.[119]

Try as I might I could not understand what I was doing. I had degrees in theology and spirituality. I had preached exegetically through the entire Bible.

---

[119] Romans 7:1-4

Paul said the same thing. "I do not understand what I do. For what I want to do, I do not do, but what I hate I do… For I have the desire to do what is good, but I cannot carry it out."[120]

Some part of us wants, maybe even needs, to do these things. The Nobel Prize-winning scientist Michael Polanyi showed, there are objective truths that can only be known subjectively.

How can we know unconditional love unless we have actually failed? When Martin invited me to preach, even though he knew others would call and take exception, that was one of my lessons in unconditional love.

My brother says change happens with time and effort, but transformation only occurs after something has died. Paul said he was dead to the law. It is not that the old code doesn't apply, it just doesn't have power any more. No power to motivate through either inspiration or fear, and once that is gone a person is left looking.

I can see the logic of a moral life, it's obvious to anyone who can put two and two together. It seems a better way to live. The fact of the matter though is that it doesn't give what we long for most deeply. If you save diligently you probably will have a lot of money eventually, but in the end, so what? All the pieces can be put in the right place and yet something still lacks. Eventually life brings a series of circumstances that overwhelm all the precious causes and effects we held to so dearly. Almost no one makes it past mid-life with all their convictions intact.

When the bible talks about faith in Jesus, it is talking about something more than everyday trust. Trust is based on

---

[120] Romans 7:15,18b

performance. Faith is prompted by an encounter with God and expresses itself when we give ourselves without reservation to God. When referring to faith in God, "in" is sometimes used as an accounting term; *into the ownership of.* But that kind of abandon is also a mark of intimacy when we give ourselves completely to another.

"I am my beloved's and my beloved is mine," Solomon said in his love poem.[121]

> When we are one with Jesus in faith, we have
> ...died to the law through the body of Christ...
> Therefore, there is now no condemnation for those who are in Christ Jesus, because through Christ Jesus the law of the Spirit who gives life has set you free from the law of sin and death.[122]

"Thanks be to God," Paul said. "There is no more condemnation and the life we live is empowered by the Spirit and not by obligation."[123]

This is not an intellectual explanation but an encounter. We don't know freedom from condemnation and unconditional acceptance without actual failure. The fruit of a good life grows from there. The post-moral man is beyond the reach of the law. It still describes what is good, but the post-moral man in neither motivated nor condemned by the law. He's free!

So why does the bible say in some places that the law of God is nourishing, transforming and life-giving,[124] while

---

[121] Song of Songs 6:3
[122] Romans 7:4; 8:1,2
[123] Romans 7:25-8:4 a.p.

Paul says it leads to death? The difference is obligation. When we choose God's life-rules from an open heart they are life-giving. When the moral law is an absolute and unobtainable obligation, it sucks the life out of us. The Ten Commandments make this vivid. Fundamentalists see these as demands. They were originally called the Ten Words. Ten life-giving words that begin with love. Commitment reaches beyond obligation.

Inspiration

With God, when something dies, something else comes to life.

In my last year of Bible College Mona came home from the swimming pool and her hands shook. She had seen a little girl lifeless beneath the water. A lifeguard pulled the child out but her body was motionless.

"Turn her on her side," Mona had said, and water spilled from the girl's lungs.

What the child needed was a breath. She gasped and came to life. We all need a deep breath.

I stopped breathing six weeks after my thyroid was removed. I was sleeping on the floor of the living room because I snored so badly that my wife could not rest. The usual repositioning of arms, prodding until I rolled to my side, and even sharp jabs, had failed to reset me.

I woke in the dark and the Voice said *Breathe*. I was settling back under when I heard again, *Breathe*. I did not take a breath but began counting. One-one-thousand, two-one-thousand, three-one-thousand… .I counted to forty-five, then sixty, then fifteen more after that.

---

[124] Psalm 19:7-9

Breathe...or you will die.

I thought about sleeping the endless sleep, I was that tired. But. I willed myself to draw in one deep breath. Other breaths came after that as my fingers walked to my neck and sampled the lateral scar beneath my Adam's apple. When my heart settled, I slept again. No one had remembered to prescribe the hormonal supplements I needed to go on.

I never really caught my breath spiritually. Six years after thyroid cancer, after the hormonal engine between my head and my heart had been removed, I burned out. It took more and more to do less and less, until it took everything to do almost nothing.

Previously I had found my breath on mountain hikes where vistas of glaciated peaks that touched the light blue above and deep blue sea below restored my sense of awe. After burnout, even the things that once filled me only drained me more. I didn't have even the energy to get started. Weariness can be the soil of weakness.

There is one word for both breath and spirit in biblical Hebrew and Greek. Saul was transformed and saw clearly when he was filled with God's Spirit. He was freed from his need to fulfill the requirements of the law because of what Jesus did in his life and death. Paul was empowered to live a life that was free of guilt and pleasing to God because of the ongoing presence of the divine Spirit.

The Fruit Of A Spirit-filled Life

Life with God is less like a repair manual and more like a fruit tree. Followers of Jesus have been freed from the law and filled with new life "in order that we might bear fruit for

God."[125] Paul described that fruit: love, joy, peace, patience, kindness, goodness, and gentleness; and in that cornucopia he included self-control.[126] It seems an odd fit.

The rest are qualities of spirit. In fact, Paul said they are the fruit of a life full of Spirit. All the qualities expressed, except self-control, would normally be thought to find their home in the heart. They are rooted and expressive of a person's inner being.

Love, joy, peace, patience kindness, goodness and gentleness are something more than an intellectual or volitional exercise. But for much of my life self-control has been the corollary of doing what one should, an act of the will or a steely determination that overpowers emotions and circumstances. But self-control as spiritual fruit is not like that. It is of a different species.

None of the other qualities Paul mentioned flow from what one ought to do. We do not love, or live with joy and peace, because we should. We may well be meant to live with these qualities, but they will not flow from within because we feel they must.

There is a personal quality to these fruits of the Spirit. Each reaches beyond what is moral to something spiritual. That is Paul's point, that these evidences of a Spirit-full life are not obligated, but organically inspired. What if there is a different kind of self-control?

Self-control, perhaps uniquely in this grouping, can be produced from the wrong motives. We can live with control out of fear or oppression, but it does not flow from the same inner spring that patience, kindness and goodness come from. Spiritual self-control is un-coerced.

---

[125] Romans 7:4
[126] Galatians 5:22,23

This does not mean that self-control is always easy, any more than that it is always convenient to love, or that peace is unchallenged by circumstances. What it does mean is that this kind of self-control is a deeply held internal intention before it is an external expression. The fruit might look the same as the wax copies found in wicker baskets, but one bite would tell you that it is completely different.

In his Meditations, Marcus Aurelius said:

> One man, when he has done a service to another, is ready to set it down to his account as a favour conferred. Another is not ready to do this, but still in his own mind he thinks of the man as his debtor, and he knows what he has done. A third in a manner does not even know what he has done, but he is like a vine which has produced grapes, and seeks for nothing more after it has once produced its proper fruit. As a horse when he has run, a dog when he has tracked the game, a bee when it has made the honey, so a man when he has done a good act, does not call out for others to come and see, but he goes on to another act, as a vine goes on to produce again the grapes in season.[127]

Spirit-inspired self control grows with an organic ease, rooted in conviction, watered perhaps by the tears of suffering, but growing in the sunshine of emotional warmth. That may be where I have seen these qualities before—in those who are in love. Not just the first flush, but the

---

[127] The Meditations of Marcus Aurelius, Trans. George Long, Duncan Baird Publishers, Book 5;6

assurance of mature love. That is where you find joy, peace, patience, kindness, gentleness and even self-control, in a heart that knows it is loved. That is a different kind of self-control. It is the kind that disciplines itself to do some things, and restrains itself from others, all from a full heart.

I have seen this kind of self-control too, though perhaps not so perfectly, in those with faith. I have observed adultery in my own life and others. Those who lack faith within are seldom faithful to others.

Not the abstract kind of faith, the kind with no object, but in those with concrete faith, faith like Abraham's. He didn't believe for who knows what, he believed God for a boy. Even if Abraham did try to take matters into his own hands at one point, God took them back another day on a mountaintop. It has to do with hope. The hopeless are seldom self-controlled. One will persist in some things and restrain themselves from others in the light of hope.

Of these three reasons for self-control, the greatest is love.

Post-Moral Strength

Post-moralism is not amoral or immoral. It is a matter of motive power. One half of that is the heart-condition, the other half is all about strength.

If strength is a virtue how do we foster and train it? Sometimes through exertion, other times with rest. Sometimes with nourishment, and other times with moderation. I grew up in a culture that venerated brokenness and weakness as opportunities for God's strength.

"When I am weak, then I am strong,"[128] Paul said.

---

[128] 2 Corinthians 12:11

Weakness and brokenness, however, are starting points for new health and strength. They were never meant to be the ultimate goal. I grew up hearing about the need for a broken will. There are benefits to being broken, but I can't think of any benefits from staying broken. The saints may have been shattered at points, but they had iron wills. They argued and fought with God and others. They persisted when everyone else had fallen away. Their motives were misunderstood and at times their actions were misguided but, oh, were they tough. Samson fought a thousand. Jacob wrestled with God. David fought a giant. Paul endured beatings and prison. They stumbled but would not stop.

Practically

"That was a great sermon," people sometimes said after I preached.

"How will you apply it?" was my usual response.

After studying, pondering and living through much of what Paul wrote about transformation, how will I apply it and take the next step? One could apply the principles of post-moral living to any aspect of life. My issue has been sex. I could stop here and avoid the risk of giving too much information. But I know that virtually all men and many women struggle with the same issue. What I want is intimacy and passion. What arises in their absence is lust.

These are my options: a. occasional intimacy, b. celibacy, c. marriage. Let me start with the last first.

Marriage. There have been two types of advice on this. One group has told me I am never allowed to marry again because of my adultery. Another group says marriage is the cure.

101

For those who have married and failed, or maybe paired more than once and parted, it is increasingly difficult to find a compatible partner. By mid-life we have lost the optimism that enabled us to embrace our spouse with hope in the early years. We know who we are and see more clearly who others are too.

Paul said it is better to marry than to burn.[129] It strikes me as a terrible reason to marry. Imagine telling a woman you want to marry her because you don't want to lust. Women usually want to inspire desire, not quench it. I wonder too whether it is really a good idea to take advice on sex from a man who was chained in prison and could count his friends on one hand. Still, for the first time in my life I am seriously considering celibacy.

Celibacy. Abstinence from sex is not deliverance from desire. The early desert father Anthony the Great said a man can escape every temptation in the desert, except lust. I left an immoral relationship, but the desire remained within me. I know this: it is possible to abstain from sex and yet burn all the hotter. I know my limit. After a protracted time without sex, the body, mind and emotions become agitated. Intimacy restores clarity, productivity and peace.

There are sexless marriages. She's not going to give him any while he treats her so badly. He can't see any reason to treat her well while she's so cold. Things spiral downward. Sometimes desire has vanished because of stress. The medication for depression can reduce desire. Prostate cancer can end things. Sexual celibacy generally doesn't work for one partner or the other in a marriage.

---

[129] 1 Corinthians 7:9

I have lived on my own for more than four years now. Loneliness is gradually emptying me. The lack of intimacy, and the sexual substitutes that take its place, are hollowing me out. Still, why have most of the great spiritual leaders of the world chosen celibacy; even when it meant leaving their families. What did Jesus, Gandhi, the Buddha and Paul all know that I don't?

Occasional intimacy. I used to call this casual sex and was unequivocally opposed to it. That's easier to stand against when you are married and making love five times a week. I'm not saying occasional intimacy is moral. There are compelling societal, psychological and physical reasons against it. But I know too that there have been sincere encounters that brought life and comfort to both partners. Conversation was meaningful; there were shared values and interests. Sometimes it is easier to begin a relationship when you have no preconceived expectations.

Whatever the path ahead, I need to be transformed.

A New Life

Post-moralism is where one finds oneself when one is dead to the obligations of the law yet still hopes for goodness. The law, and the fear it generates, are no longer the motivation. One may or may not yet be dead to sin. Given time, sin produces its own discontent or disgust and can prompt a repentance from "things that lead to death."[130]

The turning to life is a different matter. In the post-moral person, hope and strength come not from fear or even determination, but through a personal encounter with the divine Spirit. It is not informational but experiential, relational

---

[130] Hebrews 9:14

and transformational. It is the work of the Spirit. Whether in the life of Moses, David, Paul, Peter or any other, it is God who brings life and a righteousness apart from the law.[131] There is not a single incidence of repentance in the Bible apart from the presence of God in word, spirit, or personally. The new life is pursued from the inside out. It is free of shame and fear and lives from the love of God and with kindness for oneself and for others.

I was nearly done writing this chapter when I thought I should look up the biblical definition of morality. There isn't one. The words moral, morals, and morality are not used in the bible. ("Moral" is used in James 1:21 (NIV) to modify "filth", but "moral" is not in the original language.) I have lived most of my life trying to be something the bible never mentions. I thought that if I was a moral man, if I lived morally, God would be pleased with me. God doesn't even use the word. "What are you talking about?" he responds to my one-sided conversation. How freeing is that!

There are thirty-six references in the Bible (NIV) to immorality. All of them are about sexual immorality.[132] Almost all of those use a form of the Greek word *porneia*, the root of our word pornography.

In the teaching of Jesus about adultery, not only the act is sin. The lust that ignites with a look and burns in the heart defiles a man.[133] It is proof of unbelief. Stricter rules and more effort are not the cure. The absence of faith is the root of sexual immorality.

---

[131] Romans 3:21-28
[132] 32 explicit references in English while the other 4 are clearly about sexual immorality in the original language.
[133] Matthew 5:27,28

If the bible does not talk about morality, it does speak of holiness, righteousness, and goodness. The source of holiness is not obligation, but intimacy. Rules can't create that. When the Spirit of God penetrates our lives, when God surrounds us in his presence, there is no condemnation but righteousness, holiness and goodness.

On the way back from Rwanda there was a twelve-hour layover in London. Once clear of customs at Heathrow, we boarded a train to the centre of the city and walked to Westminster Abbey.

You cannot take a step in that church without treading on someone. Thirty-three hundred bodies are buried in the walls, in specially erected chapels and everywhere under the floor. From Edward the Confessor to Mary Queen of Scots to Cromwell—who was disinterred by Charles II for executing Charles I. Cromwell's long-dead body was hung and decapitated at Tyburn Gallows and his head set on a pole outside Westminster Hall. There is a chiseled reminder of where Cromwell used to be buried.

The bodies of Dickens, Newton and Livingstone are kept in the Abbey too, along with others poets, politicians, people of accomplishment and one man who lived through ten kings and lasted one hundred and fifty-four years. Somewhere on that floor it struck me that only two weeks before I had been in a nameless church in Ntarama, where bodies, clothing and blood were still splashed over low wooden benches. Now, I was in one of the most famous churches in the world, walking among the bodies of the rich, powerful and famous, and all of them were just as dead.

In the train on the return to the airport five engineers from Asia sat across the aisle and asked where we had been.

"Rwanda."

"Why?"

We told them we had gone on a mission of peace and reconciliation.

"What makes you think you can make any difference?" one of the engineers asked.

"Resurrection," I said. No hesitation. "I believe in Resurrection."

That is the gift of God's Spirit and my hope. Not just life after *the* death, but after the many deaths that come to every life given time.

6. Friend Of Sinners

Jesus likes those who are not so good more than those who think they are.

"There's good news and there's bad news," the angel said. "Which do you want first?"

"Give me the good news," the man replied.

"You know that person who cheated and betrayed you?" the angel asked, and the man nodded. "God *really* loves that person. They're close friends."

I thought you were going to give me the good news first!"

"Good news, bad news, it's the same," the angel said.

"You told me my worst enemy is God's close friend. How is that good news?"

"His worst enemy is God's good friend too."

God With Us

I miss Christmas.

I remember placing the tree in a playpen so our two year old could not get at the decorations and then watching as he found a broom and swiped at them anyway. I remember shopping for the tree as a family and arguing over which was best until we began rotating the final choice from person to person each year and pretended to argue after that. Sixteen footers filled the tall space in the centre of the home we had built on a hill. I remember piling gifts under the tree and taking turns opening them from youngest to oldest. I remember the luminaries, (candles in glowing brown paper bags with scoops of sand at the bottom to hold them in the wind) that lined the walk to the front door when I returned from church on that holy night. Every year Mona stacked the dining table with appetizers, chocolate and desserts. All of our favorites.

One Christmas I gathered bales of hay and borrowed a lifelike infant doll and trudged out to the weathered grey barn on the back of the acreage where we lived. I set the scene with straw and light and a blanket that held the meaning of the night and then retraced my steps to the house. After church and our favorite foods I told my children, wife and parents to pull on jackets, boots and gloves but would not tell them why. They followed me out and trod in the path I pressed into the foot of fresh snow that had fallen since my last visit to the barn. The moon was full that cloudless night and hung exactly over the peak of the barn. The reflected glory of moon and snow showed us the way.

"Someone's in there," my son said when he caught the glow of the candle-lantern. I pried on the sagging door and let them in. The stables were to one side and the straw was stacked where the ladder came down from the loft. The mustiness of animals long absent still lingered. The manger waited in the midst of the soft light.

I read the Christmas story from the Gospel of Luke that night and Mona mouthed some of the words. She had memorized them all as a child while watching Charlie Brown's Christmas. That night, we knew God was present. I believe God was in Bethlehem once, but Christmas has as much to do with where God is as where he was. Who could have known God would actually be with us when we stood in the mess of our old barn?

Jesus called a tax collector named Levi (also called Matthew) to follow him. Tax collectors were the bottom of the barrel in the eyes of the Jews. They were other Jews who contracted with the Romans to collect taxes, and anything they could gather over the required amount they kept. They were despised. Jesus called one to be his close disciple. Matthew invited Jesus and the other disciples for dinner. Matthew's tax collector friends wanted to know more about this Jesus and came for dinner too.

> When the Pharisees saw this, they asked his disciples, 'Why does your teacher eat with tax collectors and sinners?' On hearing this, Jesus said, 'It is not the healthy who need a doctor, but the sick. But go and learn what this means: "I desire mercy, not sacrifice." For I have not come to call the righteous, but sinners.'[134]

After that, those opposed to Jesus said he was a friend of sinners.[135] Jesus quoted them and took the title on.

The Old Testament uses a variety of words for sin. None of those words are exclusively religious as the English word sin is. They speak of missing the mark, of misdemeanors and negligence; to bend or err.[136]

No Fear

I would not be a Christian, except for the relentless attraction of Jesus. The organized church operates like any other power structure. The message and mission is one of grace, but the reality is more often present on the fringes than at the core.

---
[134] Matthew 9:11-13
[135] Matthew 11:19; Luke 7:34
[136] Quell, Theological Dictionary of the New Testament, vol. I, p.268-271

Evangelicals are not ahead of Catholics theologically, they are just behind them sociologically. Power is centralizing. The problems of pain and evil are answered in ways that are intellectually rigorous but neither compelling nor comforting. Christianity is fabulous on paper but incredibly messy in life. But, there is Jesus; there is this man who is compassionate and kind to those who are broken and hurting. He stands up to the arrogant and the oppressive and he is shrewd and smart with a touch of irony. Oh, to be like him. If being like Jesus is our goal, the life of Christ is the path.

Jesus' extraordinary life began with an unusual conception.[137] An angel told his virgin mother the Spirit of God would impregnate her. An angel also told her fiancé not to worry. Most everyone else thought predictable thoughts.

Jesus was fully divine and fully human. What if every child was received and raised as if they were at least half-divine? What if every single woman who found herself pregnant had a messenger who told her she was highly favored by God? What if every person who felt shunned by a partner they had given everything to was told the life of God was in that? Would things be different? It takes the fear out when we really believe God is in it.

However Jesus began, by the time he was twelve he had the confidence to converse with prominent religious leaders on the most religious day in the most religious place in the country. He had enough conviction that he did not need his parents' approval.[138]

---

[137] Luke 1:26-35
[138] Luke 2:41-52

In maturity, he could gently chide his mother. He had a sense of his own timing but he was flexible.[139] There is an absence in the early life of Jesus of the maxim that children are to be seen but not heard. Jesus stood up to others and for himself. Jesus had no fear.

If every parent raised their child believing they shared the divine nature, there would be less fear. My own religious tradition emphasized the opposite; the original sin of Adam and Eve passed a sinful nature on to every infant—except Jesus. Evangelical parents began with the bent that children are disposed to sin. It was believed this could be overcome by teaching and discipline. I don't believe in the innate and absolute goodness of children but corruption seems a hard place to start.

My four-year-old son came shopping with me one Christmas. When I looked up from the pots and pans I wanted to buy for his mother the boy was gone. He was not in that aisle, nor in the next. I yelled his name and other parents who understood my terror began to help. A security guard radioed to watch all the exits. After five minutes of looking and yelling another parent held my son's hand and brought him to me.

"He was playing and riding the escalator up and down."

We hugged. I cried. I took the little boy home and told him how important it was for him to listen to me and obey. I would not do it now, but then I spanked him in the hope that he would remember to stay close. When I finished, and tears still flowed from my eyes but not his, he turned to me and said, "Whew, you almost spanked the sin right out of me!"

---

[139] John 2:1-4

He knew more than I did. Fear motivates, but punishment doesn't fix us.

Life Of The Party

I did not drink. As a teenager I didn't like the taste but I poured a few beers into potted plants at parties to keep up appearances. After my wife and I tried the cheap champagne that came with the honeymoon suite we decided not to bother again given her alcoholic father.

I grew up in a teetotalling home. "Do not be drunk with wine...but be filled with the Holy Spirit,"[140] the bible said. Many Evangelicals avoided getting happy by either means. Beyond that Evangelicals had an abundance of explanations for the wine in the Bible.

It was so weak that your bladder would fail before you could ever get drunk. The wine in the Bible should have been translated grape juice or even grape jelly.

Jesus went to a wedding at Cana where the family ran out of wine—the celebration was in peril.[141] Mary the mother of Jesus told the stewards what to do.

"Do whatever he tells you,"[142] she said and then pointed to her son. What had he already done around home?

Jesus told the stewards to take six huge ceremonial jars and fill them with water. Then they took a sample to the master of ceremonies and he wondered: *Why was the best saved until last?* Everyone who has been to a party knows why that question was asked. Everyone who has lived a while hopes the water of their life can be transformed, that the best might still be to come.

---

[140] Ephesians 5:18
[141] John 2:1-11
[142] John 2:5

Wine is a symbol for life in the Bible. Not the stodgy life of a person who measures success by all the things they have not done, but a life with bouquet and depth and finish. A life that smiles at children, listens to the elderly, confronts injustice, dances with passion and sparkles with hope. Let me be that kind of man.

Fifteen years after I decided never to drink, a year after cancer, the Voice said, *Have a little wine.* I rationalized it away but when I went to my car and turned the key the radio announced the medical benefits of a daily glass of red wine. A day or two later a friend raised the topic. The Voice persisted, *Have a glass of wine with dinner.* After discussing the matter with my wife and my children, after buying two of the smallest wine glasses on the shelf, after the second trip of my life to a liquor store, I had a glass of wine. I didn't like it. I did not know yet that it is not the best idea to begin with the cheapest wine. My metabolism is better. I have more life with a little wine.

After turning water into wine Jesus went to the temple and cleaned house.[143] People filled the temple at Jerusalem trying to get close to God and some profiteered by that. The law laid down a system of sacrifices and offerings that kept things open to the poor. If you couldn't afford a lamb to sacrifice, a pigeon was acceptable. A small donation was enough from the poor. But those in authority decided that these sacrifices and offerings had to be approved. Guess who held the franchise for the approval of animals and coins? The religious leaders.

Jesus cleared them out. He made a whip of rope. He overturned tables and left moneychangers scrambling. There should be no gouging when it comes to getting close to God. I

---

[143] John 2:13-17

wish there had been pictures of that Jesus on my childhood walls instead of the doe-eyed man who looked like he wasn't sure what to do.

I wish I had overturned the table at my last meeting with the church board. I wish I had turned the table when my replacement told me I had nothing more to say; preaching really wasn't my gift. Why didn't I overturn the table? Did I think it was just about me? I knew the same things would happen to others after I was gone. What a mess there will be if I speak up, I thought. What a mess there was because I didn't.

Embracing Outcasts

Jesus met a fearful woman at a well on the edge of town in the region of Samaria.[144] Jews didn't have anything to do with Samaritans and to make matters worse this was a lone woman. Some religious Jews prayed, "Thank God that I am not a Gentile, a dog, or a woman." Religion has not always been kind to women, but Jesus was.

Jesus asked the woman at the well to get her husband.

"I have no husband,"[145] she said.

"You are right when you say you have no husband. The fact is, you have had five husbands, and the man you now have is not your husband. What you have just said is quite true."[146]

Amazing! "You're right...What you have just said is quite true." You can't embrace people like that with posturing and half-truths. Grace without truth is mush and truth without grace is harsh. Jesus was full of grace and truth. He could be good without making others feel bad. He was insightful

---
[144] John 4:4-30, 39-42
[145] John 4:17
[146] John 4:17

without making others feel stupid. For someone who came to save the world from sin, he didn't make a big deal of it. Jesus didn't make pronouncements on sin or teach his disciples a doctrine of sin. He offered no speculations and not once did he define sin. Jesus didn't tell sinners what must be said, but he takes the awkwardness out of expressing our need to God.[147] He inserts hope where most of us lean to guilt or shame.

While I was still in the upper echelon of ministers in my city I was asked to preach at the Gospel Mission downtown. The chapel was full when I arrived; anyone who wanted dinner had to listen first. The water was wide between my shore and theirs but after I finished a woman came forward and asked me to pray for wisdom for her. Two different men had invited her to live with them and she didn't know which one to choose.

"I don't need to pray. I know the answer," I said.

"You do?" she said with surprise.

"Yes. You shouldn't live with either of them."

Her lips curled down and she said "I didn't need to ask a little fuck like you to get an answer like that."

Ten years later my youngest son and I parked in front of a grocery store in the West End of Vancouver after building a float to represent the homeless shelter he worked at in the Pride parade. Before we got to the door a young woman wrapped a big hug around my son. She talked about her trip to Alberta to see her dad and her kids, about the loss of her husband, about the need for a place to stay. Her boyfriend came out of the grocery store and shook our hands. They told

---

[147] Rengstorf, Theological Dictionary of the New Testament vol. I p.329, 330

of the sharp-dressed man who had seen them panhandling and bought them sandwiches, smokes and even dog-food for the small bundle of fur that was sitting on the sidewalk. The man had paid with a hundred dollar bill and gave them a twenty from the change. The generous man had lost his partner recently.

"I can understand that," the woman said. "All of a sudden my husband was gone."

The woman and her boyfriend were tenting in Stanley Park and asked if they could get bedding from the temporary shelter where my son worked graveyard shifts.

"Sorry but we have to hold on to that," he said.

"I have a sleeping bag you can have," I interjected.

It was a leftover from some I had given away.

"I'll give it to my son and you can pick it up from the shelter," I said. I didn't want them to know where I lived. After they left I commented that she had made a pretty quick turnaround with her husband gone.

"Stanley Park isn't that safe at night, Dad," my son said. "She needs someone to keep her safe."

I had never considered that when I offered my glib advice to the woman at the Gospel Mission. I am learning to lose my arrogance and look behind the superficial.

The woman who met Jesus at the well did not go and get her husband. She went and got the village.

"Come, see a man who told me everything I ever did. Could this be the Messiah?"[148]

Truth and Spirit came together in a life-giving way. The village came to Jesus to encounter someone who knew

---

[148] John 4:29

everything about the most colorful woman in town. But like every one of us who hopes to be both known and loved, they came to see for themselves. Life is very different once we move beyond fear and blame.

Sight For The Blind

Who sinned? That is the question most of us ask when something has gone wrong.

"Who did something wrong? Was it this man or his parents who sinned?" the disciples asked as they looked at a man born blind.

"Neither," Jesus said. "He's this way so God can show everyone how He works."[149]

That's a different perspective. I grew up in a home where someone had to be responsible if something went wrong. I carried that approach with me when I left. When my work as a minister ended, I had to blame someone. When my marriage ended, I had to blame myself. It's true, there often is someone responsible, but there need not be blame. We can look instead for the opportunity. *What's God doing here?*

With the blind man before him, Jesus spat on the ground, made mud with the saliva, and pressed it on the man's eyes. Strange business. The blind man probably thought nothing of it. He couldn't see what Jesus was doing. It's not like he might have gone blind from it. He'd have felt it though. I have had sand in my eyes. I had stitches all around the new cornea that was sown into my left eye when the old one became corrupted and blistered and scarred. Every blink was uncomfortable for six months as the wound healed.

---

[149] John 9 author's paraphrase

Why did Jesus put dirt on the man's eyes? Who knows? But it had everyone's attention. Jesus told the man born blind to go wash in the pool of Siloam. He did, and went home seeing!

Like every miracle, some believed and others explained why it could not be.

"It's not the same guy," they said.

"Its me!" he said.

"Then how did it happen?"[150]

He described the mud in his eyes, the pool, the man they called Jesus.

"Where is this man?"[151] his neighbors asked.

"I don't know," he said.[152]

The religious leaders got hold of the story and shook it like a rag in a dog's mouth. There were rules. Jesus had healed the man on the Sabbath and the religious commentators said that wasn't allowed because it was work. The most anyone was allowed to do was to keep a situation or crisis from getting worse. Nietzsche was right. Morals are often a mask so those in power can keep others in line. The religious rulers asked the blind man's parents what had happened, but his parents skirted the issue for fear of expulsion from the community. Churches use the same weapon.

When the rulers called for the man born blind and told him Jesus was a sinner, he replied to them, "Whether he is a sinner or not, I don't know. One thing I do know. I was blind but now I see!"[153]

---

[150] John 9:8-10 a.p.
[151] John 9:12
[152] John 9:12
[153] John 9:25

They insulted the man and told him he was steeped in sin at birth.

"How dare you lecture us?"[154] they said, and then they threw out the man who could see.

Who are you to teach us anything? It is the same arrogance that makes many Christians so unattractive to the world. Evangelicalism isn't three centuries old yet we have presumed to tell Hindus and Buddhists and others, with their own stories of personal encounters with God, that they have nothing to teach.

I had dinner with a woman who would not take a glass of wine.

"Is that from principle?" I asked.

"I was sitting in the bathtub one evening with my second glass of wine when I asked if this was what my life had become." It seemed there had often been more than two glasses of wine.

"What did you do?" I asked.

"I called out to God," she said. She knew nothing of my own religious background.

"And what did God do?"

"He answered."

Her conversation with God was ongoing. She began attending a support group that met in a church basement and found a community. She tried church once. "But there was no life upstairs."

I told this story to my mother.

"Did she invite Jesus into her life?" she asked. That was the protocol we were taught; we measured conversion by a formula rather than a relationship.

---

[154] John 9:34

Jesus found the sighted man and introduced himself fully. "For judgment I have come into the world, so that the blind will see, and those who see will become blind."[155]

"You're not seeing things clearly," a minister friend of mine said when I described my disillusionment.

"At least I know that," I said.

I am quite sure I am not seeing things perfectly now. But in my blindness I have come to see Jesus more clearly.

We are all born blind. Those are the people God works with. There's no need for blame. See it as an occasion for glory.

Life Beyond Death

Jesus could be ruthlessly good. His friend Lazarus was sick; really sick.[156] Lazarus had two sisters, Mary and Martha, who were as different as hand lotion and dish detergent. But both were worried.

Mary was the woman who poured expensive perfume on Jesus and dried his feet with her hair. A lack of inhibition is a wonderful thing in a pure direction. Martha was the sister who had been busy in the kitchen the last time Jesus visited. That time she asked Jesus to tell Mary to help instead of just visiting with him.

"Mary has chosen what is better, and it will not be taken away from her,"[157] Jesus said.

You have to be at home with each other to say things like that.

---

[155] John 9:39
[156] John 11:1-44
[157] Luke 10:42

Now, Lazarus was sick, really sick. Mary and Martha sent word, but Jesus waited two more days.

"This sickness will not end in death,"[158] Jesus said to his disciples, but it did lead to death.

"Our friend Lazarus has fallen asleep; but I am going there to wake him up."[159] Jesus said.

When Jesus and the twelve arrived Lazarus had already been gone four days. Martha met Jesus at the edge of town.

"If you had been here, my brother would not have died. But I know that even now God will give you whatever you ask."[160] Oh, for love that frank, for frankness that trusting.

Evangelicals ask, "Have you been saved?"

Saved. The same Greek word is used in the Bible for salvation and healing. Greek has many more tenses than English. Of all its uses in the New Testament a little more than half the time the word is used to say we *are being* saved. A little less than half the time it is used to say *we will be* saved. Twice, just twice, the word is used to say we *have been* saved. Have you been healed? Salvation is not some end of life rescue, it is an eternity of growth.

There is a sickness unto death. Fifteen years ago the phone rang.

"Reverend Schroeder, this is Doctor Laslo. Your biopsy tested positive. The tumor is malignant."

"Cancer?"

"Yes. The surgeon's office will call you."

The bottom fell out. My first life was about to end, but it was not a sickness unto death. It was a transforming opportunity, but I didn't think that then. People prayed. I

---

[158] John 11:4
[159] John 11:11
[160] John 11:21,22

must have heard a hundred cures for cancer. I was terrified. I prayed. The Voice said, *You will go through this. But I'll be with you.*

Cancer of the type I had kills very few. It was the aftermath I was unprepared for. With the loss of my thyroid the old me was gone. My emotional stability, my quick thinking and strong will all ebbed away. On the walk to church one Sunday morning I became angry as I thought about the set-up and sound system. *No one has even done anything wrong,* I realized. *You will not correct anyone for anything today,* I instructed myself. I tried running budget numbers through my head as I walked and I couldn't. Was I going to be stupid the rest of my life?

I tried disciplining myself to work harder but fell behind. I tried to be patient, but often simmered. How much of what I assumed was intelligence and good character was merely the right blend of hormones? I considered returning to simple carpentry, but I didn't have the energy. It took six more years for me to acknowledge that the person I had been was gone. By then I had lost my vocation, my marriage, my money, much of my family, and my eyesight too. You don't have to physically die to end a life, but I came close. My own strength worked against me. The old me died before the new me came to life. It was painful.

Jesus wasn't afraid of pain. Neither his own, nor others. He wasn't afraid of being hurt, and he wasn't afraid to hurt others for a great reason.[161] He wasn't afraid to feel bad. How many of our ills are tied to the fear of pain? Sometimes, ruthlessness is required to be truly good.

---

[161] John 11:4,15

"I am going to wake Lazarus up,"[162] Jesus said.

Where is God waking me up?

Jesus let Lazarus die because he knew something good was ahead. Mary and Martha didn't. Lazarus didn't. We're fools when we pretend we do. That's not faith. When Jesus saw the sisters he was troubled. When he got to the graveside, Jesus wept. Hope doesn't take away the pain.

There's that fearlessness again. Jesus was unafraid to feel bad.

As I prepared to leave the woman I had left my wife for, my therapist guided me to that place where fear and pain burned hottest in my life.

"I know it's like putting your hand on a hot stove, but don't pull away. What do you see there?"

What I saw brought no comfort. It did bring clarity; I was afraid of rejection. Perfect love doesn't cast out the hurt, it casts out the fear of hurt.

Jesus stood by the grave and told others to roll the stone away from the mouth of the sepulcher.[163]

"But Lord," Martha said (practical woman that she was), "there's going to be a stink."[164]

There always is a stink when we get close to those who have lost their lives. Divorce, bankruptcy, substance abuse, depression, death. Death is so very messy. The life that comes after death is too. Jesus is the friend of those in a mess. The bible says we're all dead in our sin,[165] in our failure to get it right. We all need God to show up with words of life.

---

[162] John 11:11 a.p.
[163] John 11:38-44
[164] John 11:39 a.p.
[165] Ephesians 2:1

"Come out!" Jesus kept saying. "Lazarus! Come out!"[166]

It is time to come out of the tombs we have called home.

Lazarus woke up and walked out wrapped in the strips of cloth and sticky spices he had been buried in.

"Take off the grave clothes and let him go,"[167] Jesus said.

The time has come to help people free from the things they wrap around themselves in attempts to deal with what has died. Those old clothes only restrain our new lives.

I went to a twelve step meeting with a friend who was telling her story. At the end of the meeting the leader asked if anyone was getting their one-year cake for sobriety. A few stood and everyone clapped.

"Anyone at six months?" the leader asked and more stood to applause and cheers.

"One month?" More rose and then…

"Any comebacks?"

Everyone knew he meant those who had fallen and that this night was their first step back. No one stood but he called again.

"Any comebacks?'

Three men stood but their heads hung and their shoulders slumped.

Then the room erupted! Cheers, shouts and whistles bounced off the church basement walls. Shame was washed out the door.

"How do you do that?" I asked my friend. "How do you eliminate the shame?"

---

[166] John 11:43
[167] John 11:44

"It's only a shame if you don't come back," she said.

While in Rome I visited the Borghese Galleria for the third time. There was a Caravaggio exhibit. The first painting was a huge canvas of the Raising of Lazarus. Friends hold his reviving body and one arm hangs down to the earth while the other reaches up. That's where most of us find ourselves caught, between death and life.

Jesus holds out his hand to Lazarus. Some of the crowd are looking at Lazarus, but light is flowing from behind Jesus and more are looking to the source of the light. I walked closer to the canvas to see more clearly. The knuckles on Jesus hand are skinned, like a man who had been in a fight, a fight with death.

Caravaggio would know. He was a brawler who eventually killed a man. He knew about fighting and death from the other side. That's why Caravaggio didn't keep painting bowls of fruit and vases of flowers. His are the deep dramas of choice and conflict and loss and remorse. His own conflicts enabled Caravaggio to paint Matthew sitting at a table counting his money as Jesus called him. It was Caravaggio's doubt that empowered him to paint Peter upside down on a cross looking across a chapel to the glorious conversion of Paul. The look on Peter's face says *How did I get here, when I started there?*[168] It was Caravaggio's struggles that equipped him to paint Lazarus between life and death, between what we are and what we hope to be. There is new life, but it comes after the old way of living is finished.

I would not go back.

---

[168] Caravaggio was commissioned to paint both works for the chapel in the church of Santa Maria del Popolo.

With Us In The Mess

Jesus washed his disciples' feet at the very end of his life.[169] He knew the time "had come for him to leave this world and go to God the Father...Jesus knew that the Father had put all things under his power, and that he had come from God and was returning to God."[170] There was nothing to gain, nothing to prove and nothing to lose. So, Jesus "got up from the meal, took off his outer clothing, and wrapped a towel around his waist. After that, he poured water into a basin and began to wash his disciples' feet, drying them with the towel that was wrapped around him."[171] When Jesus' sense of power and security was complete, he served in the most humble of ways.

Simon Peter questioned Jesus; said *No* to having his feet washed. Peter had said *No* before; when Jesus said he was going to Jerusalem to suffer and die. When Peter said *No* that time, Jesus said, "Get behind me Satan."[172] The man who declared Jesus was the Messiah is also the one Jesus called his adversary. Do we love deeply enough to tell those closest to us that sometimes they are an adversary to our highest purpose? To say "Get behind me!" and yet still love?

"You do not realize now what I am doing, but later you will understand," Jesus said. "Unless I wash you, you have no part with me."[173] Our dirt doesn't alienate us from God. Only the refusal to be washed does that.

---

[169] John 13:1-17
[170] John 13:1,3
[171] John 13:4,5
[172] Matthew 16:23, Mark 8:33
[173] John 13:7,8

I was eating in a Roman restaurant, years after I was long gone from the church, when I saw a woman who saw into me.

"You have the eyes of a man who was blind, but now you can see," she said. I had not told her of my operations or my change of vision. Could this be the one who knew everything about me? I saw into her wounds too.

"You'd think I would have known better," she said after describing some of her relational choices.

It makes no difference when we do know better. That kind of knowledge is not the key to transformation. How did Jesus know he came from God and was going to God? How did he know God had put everything under his power? Did he read about it? Did it take practice? Was it prayer? There are truths we know only through intimacy.

Months passed and I met the woman who saw into me again in Rome. She had walked all day and after dinner we danced alone on the banks of the Tiber. She came home with me but at the door she said, "My feet are dirty, I didn't have time to bathe. They smell."

She sat on the edge of my bed and tugged at her boot but it would not come free. After I pulled off one boot and then the other, I went to the bathroom, soaked a towel in hot water, and draped a dry one over my shoulder. I knelt and wrapped one foot and then the other in the warm folds of the moist towel. I stroked the cloth over her ankles, arches and slender toes until they were fresh. Only then did I think of Jesus. Is there any way to live intimately without the tenderness that washes one another?

The night Jesus washed the disciple's feet, he said one of them would betray him. They questioned who it might be.

Within a paragraph, the current of conversation switched to a dispute over who was the greatest.[174] That was when Peter said confidently that he wouldn't let Jesus down. After Jesus assured Peter that he would fail, Jesus looked beyond the failure with Peter.

"When you have turned back," Jesus said to Peter, "strengthen your brothers."[175]

Even before Peter's big failure, Jesus believed Peter would make it. The difference in focus is profound. Jesus' concern at the loneliest time of his life is not for his friend's success, but for his friend's faith; for his ability to keep leaning into love, even after a monumental failure.

A great challenge facing the first century church was the issue of apostasy. Under Roman rule, people were expected to swear allegiance to Caesar as Lord. It was largely a political oath but many Christians refused. As Christianity grew, they were threatened with death if they would not deny Christ. Some were sown into bags and thrown into the arena to be devoured by wild animals. Others were dipped in tar and tied to poles in Nero's grounds. They were lit on fire and served as torches for his party. Those who denied Christ were called apostates.

Some regretted their apostasy and asked to return to the church. Many of the faithful were adamant that once one had turned their back on Christ there could be no return. I can imagine a broken-hearted apostate coming to Peter: "I denied Jesus... is there any way back?"

After the death of Jesus, Peter went back to fishing. What else did he know? While out in the boats Peter saw a man on the shore cooking fish on a fire of coals. When Peter

---

[174] Luke 22:24
[175] Luke 22:32

saw who it was he jumped from the boat and made his way to shore.

"Simon, do you love me with all your heart?" Jesus said.

"I'm your friend," Peter replied.

"Do you love me sacrificially, Peter?"

"I have real affection for you."

"Simon, do you care for me?"

"You know everything. You know I care for you."[176]

The over-worked confidence that once characterized Peter was gone. His unconditional belief in his success was absent. He was real. What's left is love.

Jesus, the friend to sinners, the one who is living water to a thirsty woman at a well, the one who gives sight to a man who has never seen, the one who invites a corrupt man to join his mission, the one who brings life where there is death, the one who washes the dirt from those who have failed, that same Jesus told Peter to feed and take care of his followers. Then Jesus told Peter what most of us fear. Life's going to get harder, not easier.[177] Finally, Jesus ended where he began with Peter.

"Follow me!" Jesus said.[178]

---

[176] John 21:15-17 a.p.
[177] John 21:18
[178] John 21:19

7. Shaking The Dust Off

The dust of the past clung to me. I never learned to leave. My therapist called it an adaptive disorder; an inability to get over it. I was like a carpenter with a hammer but no saw. So I kept pounding away believing that perseverance was a sure way to character and success and love. That is mostly true.

Perseverance enables children to learn the violin. It empowers businesspeople to create companies or couples to thrive beyond difficulty and boredom. But what got you where you are may not take you farther. Perseverance can destroy you too.

When Jesus sent his disciples out, he told them if they were not welcome somewhere, to shake the dust off their feet as they left.[179] The Apostle Paul had a similar way of dealing with rejection.[180] From city to city he spoke and taught until people had had enough. His welcome rarely lasted. More often, he was argued against, slandered, imprisoned, beaten, and threatened with death. By the end of his life he could count his friends on one hand. Paul's response was not, as is popular today, to say that people were misguided or that their violence was unintended. He shook the dust from his feet.

That our feet get dirty should be no surprise. For the first half of life it may be possible to cling to the ideal of relationships that are pure and clean, but reality is messy. Even the best of friends walk through disappointment and disillusionment. In a culture of clean socks and daily baths we don't understand how most of the world has walked through

---

[179] Matthew 10:14; Mark 6:11; Luke 9:5
[180] Acts 13:51

history. Around the warm belly of the earth where most of humanity lives, feet are bare or sandaled and un-insulated from the everyday dirt of life. Idealism can work against you.

Shake the dust off. I am borrowing the phrase. In the Bible, shaking the dust off one's feet had everything to do with people's response to the kingdom of God. Jesus sent disciples out with instructions to heal people and free them from demons; they were to tell people the kingdom was near. Before we shake the dust from others off, it is worth asking: Am I a healthy influence? Do I help people find freedom from their demons? I am extrapolating from God's terms for walking away to our own. As with everything, judge for yourself and keep what is good.

Why shake the dust off?

> Whatever town or village you enter, search there for some worthy person and stay at their house until you leave. As you enter the home, give it your greeting. If the home is deserving, let your peace rest on it; if it is not, let your peace return to you. If anyone will not welcome you or listen to your words, leave that home or town and shake the dust off your feet.[181]

It's time to leave when:
- You're not welcome.
- There's no peace.
- Nobody's listening.
- They're undeserving.

---

[181] Matthew 10:11-14

They're all signs of being devalued.

"Don't you get it?" my therapist asked after I had been trying for four years to make a life with the woman who had been my mistress. "She doesn't value you." It was worse than that. I didn't value myself.

I'm on my own, I thought. That felt terrifying—and then it seemed better. Sometimes it's not that we're unvalued, but that we live from very different values. When we have no value to those we're with, when we are fundamentally rejected, the best thing we can do is to shake the dust off our feet on the way out the door.

The need to know why we are undervalued only makes things stickier. There is no sense in asking why. Intellectual analysis seldom brings emotional comfort. Does it matter why? Move on.

When is it time to shake the dust off?

When you find clarity, it's time to move on. We know intuitively and almost immediately if something is life-giving or life-taking. But sometimes we persevere because we believe there should be a rational reason for withdrawal. Your emotional insight, your gut, is almost always right, as right as your reasoning. Don't be like the man who looks at himself in the mirror and then forgets to wash his face.

Action creates clarity. We live in an age of relational philosophers. We read and think about love and relationships but we live alone. We reason that if we could adjust our attitude, change our approach, we would be ready for love. We are hungry souls fiddling with recipes on paper. Better to get into the pot and turn up the heat. Conflict will produce either intimacy or clarity. Action delivers us from fear. We may not find what we want, but we discover a way ahead when we take action.

A good question creates clarity. Sometimes we founder because we are asking the wrong question. Though not everything can be concise, rephrase your questions for clarity. Instead of asking *Why don't they like me?* ask *What do we need for this to work?*

Instead of *When will I get what I want?* ask *What can I contribute to create change?*

Instead of *When will this end?* ask *How will I know I'm done here?*

One posture is passive while the other is active. What question would bring the clarity you need?

I should have known better than to have an affair. I did know better. Why, when we know better, do we not live better? The reason is seldom intellectual, but emotional, and usually tied to fear.

There are less analytical ways of knowing when it is time to go. My brother and his best friend meet on Friday nights in the man-cave to eat great slabs of meat, drink dark beer and discuss the irascible questions of life while smoking Cuban cigars. One piece of fruit picked from a branch of their thoughts is that all of our experience can be divided into two categories: things that fill us with life and things that drain us. If you are living with a net loss, eventually something dies.

Life-giving does not mean easy. A good friend and I helped a woman with limited income by replacing her hot water tank. The water shut-off valve was under the house and at the opposite end from the entrance to the dirt crawl space. We debated who would climb under and my friend pulled on some coveralls. There wasn't much space and he would have to crawl on his belly. Once he was in position to measure the length of pipe needed, I asked him, "How far is it from the ground to the bottom of the floor?"

"That depends," he said.

"On what?"

"On whether you measure from the bottom or the top of the cat turds."

A bad job can be energizing with good company. You won't want to walk away from a mess when the people you're with are great.

There are, however, people and tasks that deplete us. We need not blame them, or even ourselves. It may just be a bad fit.

If someone is part of the dark triad, narcissists, sociopaths, or psychopaths, either run for your life or be prepared to stand with strength. If it's just you, you may want to move on. If others, like children, are involved you may need to stand. Nice means nothing here. Power is everything. When my mother was a child she and her friends would hold hands and walk up to the electric fence. Whoever was at the end of the line would be shocked. When we hold on to those who refuse responsibility for their own lives we are in for some shocks. When we take responsibility for another's life we can become co-dependent, or even co-narcissistic.

Take this insight with moderation. Commitment, persistence and patience are integral to every success. If we do not know when to stop, when to walk away, the very qualities that enable us to thrive most of the time will drive us deeper into failure and dissolution. There is a time to quit.

At another level I wonder why it is the purest of loves when God pursues the most messed up, and grieves when they are lost or betray him, but when I pursue these same people, it is dysfunctional. Do I do it because of my own flaws while God is perfect? Is it because I am needy while God is not? Then just why is it that God pursues people like me? "Because love covers over a multitude of sins."[182]

The perspective of others can bring clarity. A friend who had been part of the last church I pastored invited me for drinks. His marriage had failed too. We had both left the church, but our friendship re-connected. As we talked I told him about the ancient historian Herodotus' description of a Persian practice used for personal problem solving.

When a man had a problem his friends would gather and get him drunk. As I told the story my friend ordered another round. Once the Persian man with a problem was good and drunk, he would describe his problem to his friends without holding anything back. The friends asked questions to be sure they had all the information. Then they gave their advice. In the morning when the man was sober again, he could stick with their advice or set it aside. My friend ordered another drink for me and asked how things were.

I spoke of disappointments. Of being told my girlfriend was going to one event when she went to another. Of hearing her on the phone describing all the attention she got at a party she had planned for while telling me she was going to a funeral.

"Bullshit," my friend said.

"You don't believe me?" I asked.

"No," he said. "The way you're being treated is bullshit."

I booked the moving truck. Clarity leads to action. Not just a clear mind, but clear emotions too.

---

[182] 1 Peter 4:8

Sometimes we are turned by a harsh grace. In Steinbeck's masterpiece *East of Eden* Samuel Hamilton goes to his neighbor and friend, Adam Trask, and punches him in the head once, and then again. That's when Trask comes to his senses and stops pining for the wife who shot and left him. Sometimes we need a metaphorical hit in the head to bring us to our rightful mind.

The next step is not as hard once we have clarity.

How to shake the dust off

I'd like to think that my ability to love unconditionally has something to do with my persistent affections. However, my need to win the affirmation of the disapproving, whether women or those in authority, left me reluctant to leave and shake the dust off as I went. The fear of good-bye can tie us like laces in someone else's shoes. We end up going where they want to. When a relationship is defined by fear, the person who cares less is the one with the power. I spoke to my psychiatrist about my weakness in leaving. He paused and reflected. This is going to be good, I thought. I waited for the sage advice gained from years of training and practice.

"'There must be forty-nine more ways to leave your lover,'" he said and raised an eyebrow.

"That's it?" I asked.

"Try something else," he said.

I live with ambivalence. I know there is a time to leave; I am less certain about how to do it. What follows is an assortment of scissors and saws to cut oneself free. They work whether we made the choice to move on or others made the choice for us.

Walk toward what you really want

I spent my first four years as a Senior Minister in Cold Lake Alberta. They were good years with warm-hearted people who embraced a twenty-five year old preacher and let him lead. After four years I felt I could lead well enough, but thought my character should be better. I hadn't done anything wrong; I worked hard, loved my family, served God wholeheartedly, but I felt I should be better. I took two years to study at Regent College and completed a master's degree focused on spirituality and philosophy. Great men poured into my life. I won awards for spirituality and evangelism. I went on to my next congregation full of life and good will. I was fired ten months later.

A storm had been brewing before I ever arrived. The previous minister called after I took the job and told me about the conflicts in the congregation. I was on high ground when the lightning struck. After only two weeks a board member told me many people were upset with me for all the changes I had made.

"I haven't been here long enough to change anything," I said.

I had followed the cardinal rule of new ministers: Change nothing for the first six months. I had not yet learned that five percent of people are terminally unhappy. Those people don't need a reason to express it, just an occasion, and they love to bring others along.

After a few months the board member called through the church directory with imagined slights (I had changed the time when the choir sang in the service. The board member failed to mention that the choir director had asked me to. He asked others if they knew of anything else I had done wrong.)

There were doctrinal disagreements. When I read the denominational statement of faith he disagreed with that too.

"I never thought we should have hired you," he said. "I just went along."

Ten months after arriving I was fired in a split decision. Two weeks later the board was fired for firing me. If it sounds confusing, it was.

I lay on the couch and moped for three months. One day an earthquake rolled up the hillside and rattled the dishes and swung the light fixtures. I got up, asked myself and my wife "What would we do and where we would live if we could do anything and live anywhere?"

We moved to White Rock, an ocean-side community just south of Vancouver where we raised our kids on acreage and worked at jobs we loved. I had always wanted to plant a church and was now ten times more productive. We shook the dust off by pursuing what we truly wanted. It's tempting to step back when we've been rejected. It's a great opportunity to step ahead. Step toward what you truly want and the dust falls away.

I founded my third congregation when I was thirty-three years old. I poured myself into a rag-tag collection of fifty people that met in a car museum for the first year and grew to a community of a thousand souls over the course of a decade. I sat in hospital corridors with husbands when their wives miscarried or while cancer ate away at their bodies and their hope. I kept walking with couples who hung together after affairs. I performed weddings and blessed births. Many people served from their strengths and it was glorious to be part of something greater than any of us. If you want to walk away from the dust of the past, walk toward what you truly want and enjoy.

Loosen your grip

After five years of relentless initiative I announced to the church that I had thyroid cancer. Ironically, though I had less strength than at any time in my life, the church doubled in the next year.

"We knew you couldn't do it all and the rest of us had to jump in," one person said. Whether as a leader, a parent, or a lover, withdrawal can be a good thing. When we want others to pull ahead we often need to pull back to create space for them. I had to shake some of my own dust off, the kind that said I needed to take initiative and responsibility for everything. We all create our own dust.

My former wife had to shake my dust from her feet. I went back to the house to gather my things. My clothes were in a box. The chest of my motorcycle jacket had been stabbed and slashed. Understandable, I thought, I stabbed her through the heart. My cologne and wedding ring were in a re-sealable baggy. She got rid of paintings, sold furniture and painted the house.

"I had to clean you out of my life," she said.

Seven years later I parked in her driveway on Christmas Eve and waited for our children to come out. Through the big front window of the house I had renovated I saw my family opening presents; her new husband sat in the armchair. *I stepped out of my own life,* I whispered to myself.

As soon as the kids were in the car everything was fine. My son asked for the music player and flipped through songs and we all sang along in odd harmonies and improvised lyrics. Clever humor provoked ironic laughter. We were driving to church but none of us were so sure about that. We did know we loved each other. Children are never dust.

The good life of my former marriage is not dust either. My former wife and I talk from time to time, about our children mostly, and memories surface. The clarity that it is finished has freed us to look back. The failure, anger, shame and insecurity were dust. Family is not. Even when it doesn't look like it once did, family is not dust.

Forgive

There is another kind of leaving, the sort that is irrevocable and final.

I served the church I founded for a dozen years and then I burned out. I lacked energy, initiative and humor. A brighter face came along to lead the church and after a series of pokes and prods—"People are tired of following you… You're not really a preacher… You don't fit here any more"— I found the door.

My family has not been good at leaving the past behind. Dust clings to us as though we are statically charged. My parents, in the last season of their lives, were still rankled by a church they poured their lives into. The church cheated them out of the equity from a house my parents bought and paid for. "We'll split the equity," the church promised, but after the greatest decade of growth the church took it all.

It's not easy to get rid of those memories. It can be even harder for those committed to treating others well. The expectation of reciprocation is hard to shake. If it has not been our choice to go, the dust of rejection clings to our feet as we walk away. There is a time to shake off the dust of a bad relationship, or of a good relationship gone bad.

I shook off the guilt and shame that had clung to me on the day three of my friends asked if I had yet forgiven myself. It is easier to shake off the dust when we own our part.

Shake off the dust of disappointment. If not, resentment and bitterness will infect the wounds. Forgive those who have wronged you. Forgive yourself too. We ourselves are made from dust.

Forget, or at least don't remember

If you are unable to forget, choose not to remember. God said he would no longer bring our sinful deeds to remembrance.[183] We can't directly control what comes to mind, but we can choose to create different paths for our thoughts. When a painful or vindictive memory surfaces, there are times I choose to think of something else. Like replanted trails in the alpine north of Vancouver, when we don't walk down those neural paths the memory overgrows. The new path of thought we choose can become the default for the mind as it becomes well-worn. Sometimes, we would rather remember and feel angry than feel nothing at all. When the dust of the past begins to stir, don't dwell on it; choose to think along another path.

Change the meaning

It's often not the experience, but the meaning of it that is debilitating. A person gets fired. A spouse leaves. A relative abuses a child. When a hard memory surfaces, we can re-interpret it. Every life has hardship, it's not always about me.

On the road to Juhu Beach in Mumbai a motor-rickshaw with an oxygen tank protruding a foot into traffic pulled up beside my own rickshaw. Valve safety covers were unknown in India and I imagined the damage if a car on the far side clipped the exposed valve. In junior high school, a

---

[183] Jeremiah 31:34

similar cylinder fell, the valve broke off, and the tank rocketed through an eight inch brick wall as the pent up gas vented. In India, I hoped no one would hit the far side while we drove by.

Some people are like that. They explode into you with devastating force that leaves you wondering what you could have done to provoke such an attack. Maybe nothing at all; something hit an exposed part on the other side of their lives. The blast launched them into you. When that happens, it doesn't mean anything about us.

Take action

Action is a cure for misery. Instead of waiting for others to solve problems, the courageous person asks, "What can I do?" Others can play a role in our lives but we don't control that.

When I needed to leave a relationship behind I prayed for help. After a long wait with no answer I asked myself, *What would I do if there was no God?* It troubled me to even think that way. *I wouldn't let things go on like this*, I thought. I took the step in a new direction and time made the difference.

Even when we don't get it right we can adjust our course and keep heading for our goal. One of the key components to happiness is the sense that whatever river we are in, we are steering our own boat. Action asserts that.

There is a time for disdain

Our wounds often explain us. My father is a gentle and patient man. My brother and I only ever saw our father truly angry once, when we spoke angrily to our mother. "Even when your mother is wrong she is right," my father said. Women were always right. But they're not.

"There is a time for disdain," my son told me when I was leaving a relationship of differing values and unmet expectations. In a culture of tolerance (which I support) there is a danger of believing that if everyone else is all right, there must be something wrong with me. Tolerance doesn't always mean walking away from conflict.

Some years ago a young woman saw my name on the sign in front of the church and came to see me. She was afraid for her children. A relative had abused her as a little girl and she feared the same for her children. That woman chose to confront her abuser. It created a dust-storm in her family but it freed her from the fear and self-doubt that had clung to her.

There are many ways to leave mistreatment and rejection behind. Sometimes intuition whispers the way. Another time careful thought directs us. Serendipity can bring a collusion of circumstances to illuminate our path. Direction can be found on the pages of books we read, in the words of friends, or even enemies. Often the everyday circumstances of life resonate with a strength that draws us forward.

When we leave we need to shake off the dust of expectations. Sometimes we stay in a place or relationship because we are waiting for some sort of satisfaction before we leave. Just go.

I went back to the best house I ever built to take pictures. The current owner was not the one we had sold the house to, so I introduced myself. I told him I had built the home, and to be sure he knew, I told him where I had built a secret hiding place. He did not ask me in. He did ask where the open oak stairs that ascended to the second floor had been built.

"In the garage," I said.

"I thought one of the local shops made them," he said.

He didn't really believe me.

"I made them in the garage with a table saw and a thickness planer."

The conversation paused and I asked how things had held up.

"We had to repaint the trim."

There was a lot of trim on that house and most of it was high up.

"It's been ten years," I said.

"It was a dirty trick not to paint the fascia boards before you put them up."

I was shocked. Of all the things he could have said about the house; it's open design and hardwood floors, its expansive rooms and great views, he complained about the trim paint.

"I painted it in the garage before I put it up," I said.

"We had to get a man-lift to paint it."

I asked if he could take a picture of the inside and he did. It was time to go.

"Our family didn't live here long," I said, "but it was a good home to us."

"We heard about you," he said.

I walked away and thought, *He doesn't deserve this house. I take my blessing off this house until someone better moves in.*

I will never live in that community again. If a person who lives every day in something beautiful I built has no respect for me, why would I want to be part of that?

What about those you can't walk away from? What about the relatives, former spouses, colleagues or community members who you will have to brush shoulders with? Just because you can't get them out of your life doesn't mean you have to let them in.

Five years after I left the church I founded I met with the board once more. I had received an invitation to be part of a process of reconciliation, but was then told it was sent to me by mistake. I went anyway.

The people on the board had largely changed, but the feelings were intense on both sides. As I walked through the doors to the warehouse I had helped purchase and renovate, I remembered the words of my son just an hour earlier.

"You hold the keys to your own heart and mind," my son said. "You get to choose what you will let in and what stays out."

The ninth chapter of Luke's Gospel begins with Jesus sending out his disciples to proclaim the kingdom of God and with power to heal people. If they were not welcome Jesus told them to shake the dust off their feet as they left town. Some time later, at the end of the chapter, Jesus, James and John were leaving a village where they were not welcome because of racial and religious prejudice.

When James and John saw what was happening they asked, "Lord, do you want us to call fire down from heaven to destroy them?"[184]

Jesus rebuked his disciples and they moved on to another place.

Why is it so hard to leave without anger? We often hate and even want to hurt those who have rejected us, even as we leave.

The next time fire fell from heaven it would be a very different kind of flame. Forty days after Jesus left the earth the

---
[184] Luke 9:54

divine Spirit fell from heaven like flames and filled, transformed and empowered Jesus' disciples.

Fire fell from the sky one summer night on an RV park just south of Vancouver. Earlier that evening twelve people filled a wicker basket while the balloon above bobbed over the trailers parked more or less permanently beside the mini-golf course. On most clear days you could see the lighter-than-air machines hovering behind the arc of the Pacific coast. From time to time I heard them from my yard when the pilots applied the igniters and reheated the air to add buoyancy. It was the sound of an industrial heater, a furnace firing into a skin that was thinner than the sheets you climb between each night.

As the balloon began to rise from the grassy field things popped and hissed and flames shot out instead of up. There was no emergency shut-off valve. There seldom is in life. The wicker basket started to burn and people began to jump. Braided nylon ropes that tethered the balloon to the earth caught fire and their cauterized ends trailed to the ground. Moorings should be impervious to flames. Every life has flames.

When the ropes melted and all but four people had bailed, the balloon shot up. Two women jumped from fifty and sixty feet. That's six stories high.

"We knew we had to jump or die," one said later.

The injured women lay on the ground and cried for help as they looked up at what must come down. A husband and father who had escaped searched the ground. His wife and daughter did not jump. They rode the balloon up four hundred feet. By then the flames had burned the envelope until it was nothing more than a thin tail flailing over a falling tongue of flame.

On the ground those who saw what was coming banged on doors and dragged neighbors from trailers. Others jumped out of windows as the basket hit and propane canisters launched into nearby homes. No one on the ground was hurt.

Sometimes the only thing you can do is get out. The sooner you jump, the better.

8. God's Guidebook For Cynics

Once you have seen enough, things stop making sense. All it takes is time and honesty. *"Meaningless...Everything is utterly meaningless."*[185] said Solomon, the Israelite king who may have been the wisest man to ever live. He would know. He wrote the book on cynicism; Ecclesiastes.

I was driving over the Port Mann Bridge when a police car with flashing lights pulled into the right lane and stopped. The officer got out of the cruiser and looked over the railing of the bridge. Did someone jump? I turned on the radio just in time to hear that the high-voltage lines that crossed the Fraser River had collapsed into the water! The flood-waters from this year's runoff undercut the foundations of an electrical tower and it fell into the river and pulled three other towers down too. Power was lost; the river and three sections of highway were closed.

The farther the river of life flows the more the banks of meaning erode. A storm or flood can wash away a lot. Conventional lessons are everywhere, but when the power of those fails and the old motives no longer move us ahead, one discovers the unconventional but true.

It is worth pausing here to note that the man who wrote Ecclesiastes and most of the Bible's wisdom literature would not be allowed behind an evangelical pulpit. He did not live in the box of flawlessness. He experienced everything he could in the pursuit of wisdom and wrote that he denied himself no pleasure. How else could Solomon have discovered the way beyond cynicism?

---

[185] Ecclesiastes 1:2 author's paraphrase

These days, the Evangelical church has emptied itself of experience. There may be a few secret sinners left in leadership, but they've had to learn to preach about transparency without practicing it. Have you ever heard a minister say, "It's meaningless. None of it means anything"?

I was a pastor of the hopeful variety for more than twenty years. Then my vocation, my community, my marriage and my hope all washed away. I never knew disillusionment was the path to meaning.

Nothing Means Everything

In grade four Mrs. Pascha told us to write a page on what our lives would look like when we were forty. I imagined a family in a house with two cars and a garage. By forty-five I had the house, the job, and the advancement. I lived with insight. I was prospering.

The components of my good life were the same things the teacher of Ecclesiastes listed as meaningless. Wisdom, pleasure, accomplishment, possessions, work, and position.[186] None of these things is ultimately meaningful. One would think that at least wisdom would have lasting value but "with much wisdom comes much sorrow; the more knowledge, the more grief."[187] With pleasure nothing is accomplished, and with accomplishment nothing is ultimately gained.[188] Work and possessions will all be left behind one day; maybe to a fool.[189] Advancement doesn't really matter in the end.[190]

---

[186] Wisdom, Ecclesiastes 1:12-18; Pleasures, 2:1-3, 10a; Accomplishment, 2:4-6,10b,11; Possessions, 2:7-9; Work, 2:17-23; Position, 4:13-16
[187] Ecclesiastes 1:18
[188] Ecclesiastes 2:2,11
[189] Ecclesiastes 2:17-23
[190] Ecclesiastes 4:13-16

Longing is an integral part of joy, but why do we hunger for the things that fail to satisfy? No lesson is learned until it has been lived. No poor woman believes more money would bring less happiness. Henry Ford said he was happier as a mechanic than as the owner of an automobile empire. No lonely man believes he could be lonelier still with a beautiful woman. Intelligent people do not believe there are matters beyond their understanding. The woman on her way to the top may find no pleasure once she has reached it. We need hope, but that's not the same as certainty.

There's much we don't know. We don't know what ultimately happens. Christian certainty or even arrogance about how things will play out grates on people and contrasts with what Solomon said.

All go to the same place; all come from dust, and to dust all return. Who knows if the human spirit rises upward and if the spirit of the animal goes down into the earth?[191]

How refreshing would it be to hear a preacher say: I believe in life after death, but who really knows?

Sometimes we simply attach the wrong meaning to things.

During my last summer with Mona our boarder's sister and parents came for dinner, and his sister mentioned the hearts. She had found the heart stickers in a drawer and been reminded that for many years their mother put a heart sticker on her brother's birthday on the calendar, but not on her own. She might not have ever said anything but for the discovery in the drawer.

---

[191] Ecclesiastes 3:20,21

A few heart stickers were left on the wax paper backing even though one had been given away year after year. Without thinking much the daughter had said, "I always wanted one of those."

"What do you mean?" her Mom had asked.

"Every year I watched as you put a heart sticker on my brother's birthday but not on mine," she said. "I always wished you had a heart for me too."

"A heart for you too?" Her mom started to laugh. "The heart stickers weren't for your brother. The vet gave them to me as reminders to dose the dog with her heart-worm medication."

Sometimes things don't mean what we think.

Nothing I say or do makes any difference. That felt true for me in my last meeting as a Pastor with the board of the church I founded. My colleagues were fighting with each other. The board was listening to someone who wanted me gone. My best friend was relieved to be out from my leadership. God wasn't listening and I was finished. I doubted that anything I had done made any difference. Practically speaking, they had a point. I was burnt out and wouldn't be back to myself soon. What hurt, was that those I had burnt myself out for wanted to say good-bye.

I have been an all or nothing man throughout my life; a case study in wholeheartedness run amuck. Perhaps that is why I was frustratingly attracted to women I couldn't have every bit of. When we try to make anything mean everything, we are due for disappointment. Nothing means everything.

151

If good things don't fill our lives with meaning, the bad things of life need not drain us. They are futile too. Injustice. Oppression. The hoarding of wealth.[192]

I talked with a volunteer in the library of the oldest historical and learned society in North America; the Morrin Centre in Quebec City. The building was originally the first purpose-built prison in Canada. The pleasant volunteer also happened to be a minister. Within three sentences our conversation was on to the problem of evil: If God is loving and all-powerful why does he allow evil? I did not mention my own ministerial background.

"Evil is the cost of free will," she said.

"That's no solution," I countered.

"It brings some comfort," she said in an echo of my own words a decade earlier.

"I have been to Rwanda and met widows who watched their husbands and children butchered as they themselves were raped repeatedly and left pregnant and HIV positive." I wonder now as I am writing what personal suffering prompted the librarian's answers to the question of evil.

We hope our suffering has purpose, but evil is meaningless. There is no logical cause and no existentially satisfying explanation for the bodies still draped over the pews of a church in Ntarama or the five thousand skulls stacked in the shed beside the church. Suffering has the potential to transform us, but you won't find the meaning of life there. You will go crazy trying to find an explanation. Many believe there will be an explanation in the next life, but I don't think it will be the kind people expect; not the sort of answer that makes sense of evil.

---

[192] Ecclesiastes 5:8,9; 4:1-4; 5:10-15

God's solution for the problem of evil is not an explanation, it is presence and hope. That is why God chose the incarnation—chose to come and be with us—to be one of us. The solution to the problem of evil is not an idea, it is presence, justice, comfort, and hope. These things are all personal. They happen when people are involved.

Before speaking another evening at the Morrin Centre, a different volunteer asked if I would like to see the cells in the basement. As I stood in the four by six foot space with a low sloped ceiling he asked if I wanted him to close the bars. I said yes again.

"Shall I close the wooden door?" the volunteer asked.

These were the cells used for solitary confinement where the bars and doors would be closed almost all of the day.

"Close the door," I said.

The space was very small. The smell of damp dirt and masonry was pungent.

"Shall I turn off the light?" the volunteer asked. "That's how the prisoners lived.".

"Yes. Turn off the light," I said.

I stood in the darkness for four or five minutes. *This is how many of us live*, I thought. How could one ever understand without being here? I remembered my calling to bring good news to those who are all out, to help the broken put their hearts back together, to tell people who are trapped about freedom. To let people know there is goodness waiting ahead. All about hope.

The volunteer opened the door; I stepped out of the cell and went upstairs to speak.

Within days of my affair becoming public my daughter's friend, a recent convert, sent me a card. "Who can straighten what [God] has made crooked?"[193]

I had never noticed those words before. I had never lived them before. On my slide into the affair I sought out therapists and doctors. Nothing stopped me. There are times our psyche is wrapped and tempered like a steel spring. The pressure and heat of experience has shaped us and our responses. Walking the straight way was beyond me.

The man who had been my closest friend came to see me when my failures became public. "After all that happened we thought you would either kill yourself or have an affair," he said.

"I guess I made the better choice," I joked.

He didn't laugh.

"I get it that you had an affair," he said. "But why have you carried on? Why don't you just go back?"

I never had an answer for that.

After telling us that God makes some things crooked, the Teacher says: "Don't be over-righteous, neither be over-wise; why destroy yourself?"[194]

I was definitely not taught that! I was raised in the rare air where people believed in being "wholly sanctified." To be sanctified is to be made holy, or set apart. Most of those I knew equated holiness with being morally pure. When we try to always do what is right and try to make sense of everything, we are on the path to destruction. I never learned that relentless goodness could lead to massive failure.

Social research by Dr. Salvatore Maddi revealed that children raised to be "good" girls and boys have diminished

---

[193] Ecclesiastes 7:13
[194] Ecclesiastes 7:16

resilience. Their ability to get through difficulty and bounce back from failure is reduced. Get over it. Get over the need to be that good.

Not long ago I sat in a coffee shop and the two men at the next table drew me into their conversation.

"I just want to be wholehearted and one hundred percent pure," one man said to me.

"I don't think God cares so much about that," I said. "What if you could be eighty percent sincere? Wouldn't that be pretty good?"

We move beyond cynicism when we expect a little less.

My Dad came to one of my basketball games when I was fourteen. I had heard the stories of his basketball exploits when he was a teen and wanted to impress him. The coach knew my father was there and played me a lot. I missed free throws and turned the ball over. It was my worst game of the season.

I apologized for my poor play to my coach after the game and he said, "A ripe apple only gets rotten. But a green one keeps on growing."

"Maybe don't try quite so hard next time," my Dad said.

There is no one on earth who gets it all right. Don't destroy yourself trying. No one understands everything. Here are some things to let go of on the journey beyond cynicism.

1. Life's not fair. Just because you've been good doesn't mean life will be good to you.
2. Certainty is not faith. The truth of faith is sure, but not like 2+2=4. The more personal knowledge is, the less it avails itself of that kind of certainty. We

can live with conviction, even when we have lost certainty.
3. Life is beyond your control.
4. People won't remember the good you've done.
5. No one knows the future.

After his advice to be neither over-righteous nor over-wise, Solomon says:

> Do not be overwicked,
>   and do not be a fool—
>   why die before your time?
> It is good to grasp the one
>   and not let go of the other.
>   Whoever fears God will avoid all extremes.[195]

There are some lasting values in the book of Ecclesiastes. Hold on to these things:

1. Do everything with all your might.[196]

Herodotus the ancient historian wrote of a conversation between a Persian ruler and a captured Greek general on the eve of Persia's attack on Greece. The Greek general advised against the attack even though the Persians had more than a million soldiers.

"Your supply lines might fail because of their length, or a storm might destroy the fleet or some other disaster might befall you," he said.

---

[195] Ecclesiastes 7:17,18
[196] Ecclesiastes 9:10

The Persian ruler responded. "If the kings of Persia had thought like you we should have never accomplished anything. The best one can do is to prepare and then do the best they can. Then, even if you fail, you know it was only bad luck and not a bad plan."

It is a good perspective. Still, a storm did wipe out the fleet, another destroyed their bridge across the Hellespont and King Leonidas and three hundred Spartans turned back an army at the pass at Thermopylae.

2. Life is risky.[197]

Solomon said that if you dig a well you might fall in. If you cut down a tree it might fall on you and if you quarry stone a rock might crush you. Every home I have built required digging, cutting and heavy objects.

In a remote village in Burkina Faso I saw men digging by hand more than one hundred meters deep for water. Men died when they hit gas pockets far underground. But others kept digging. I asked why they would take such a risk but before I finished the question I knew the answer. *Life is worth the risk.*

3. Invest widely.[198]

If one thing doesn't pay off, another might. While there is power in focus, there is risk if we only ever focus on one thing.

There are times to let go. There are times to hang on.

---

[197] Ecclesiastes 10:8,9
[198] Ecclesiastes 11:2

"I will not let you go," the Voice said at the beginnings of cancer and of my affair. I could believe that. My father had said the same thing.

That story started with a squirt of water—straight up through the concrete of the basement floor! I had never heard of such a thing. We lived in Kelowna where water flows from sprinklers rather than falling from the sky. The only other time our basement had been damp was when the hot water tank blew up, and while that was exciting, the water squirting through the floor was far more mysterious.

My dad, being the pragmatist he is, decided to put a nail in to stop the leak. That worked for a while, but soon there were two other mini-geysers. I wondered if our house would sink and then my dad started digging. When we finally got to the bottom of the matter we discovered that our house was over an underground stream. We dug a sump-hole five feet deep and two feet in diameter just outside the back door and lined it with concrete pipe. Not wanting the pump to clog with dirt, dad decided we needed to line the bottom with cement pads.

Dad said he would lower me into the pipe while he held my feet so I could place the cement pads in the bottom. The water was too deep for me to hold my head out if he let go, and the pipe was too narrow for me to turn around in. If he dropped me I would be finished. Faith is not about probabilities or risk analysis.

"I won't let you go," Dad said.

Down I went—and my father never let go. I was able to do my part because I believed he had hold of me.

Even when I was faithless, God was faithful.

Everything Can Mean Something

None of the big six: wisdom, pleasure, accomplishment, possessions, work or advancement, bring ultimate meaning to life, but they all contribute something. The way past cynicism is to enjoy what life does offer.

In Taormina, on the southwest coast of Sicily, I sat with friends on their terrace looking over the Mediterranean Sea. Seven years had passed since I had left the church and my marriage. Though Michael and Rose had lived in Italy for decades, there was still nothing Michael enjoyed more on his birthday than one of his hand-fashioned hamburgers. Two thin patties were pressed together around a blend of peppers, onions and spices.

"This may be the best burger I have ever tasted," I said.

"Greg," Rose said, "Somewhere, sometime, something has to be the best. Why not let it be now?"

I laughed and concurred. "This *is* the best hamburger I've ever tasted!"

One doesn't question a delicious meal. When I have built a piece of furniture, seeing what I've done at the end of a productive day feels good. "Wisdom is better than folly, just as light is better than darkness."[199] Passionate sex with a loving partner is nourishing. Enjoyment, not analysis, is the cure for cynicism. The road from cynicism leads through tangible pleasures and accomplishment, whether the work of our hands, the food we eat, or the intimate pleasure of our mate. None of these can be denied or explained away. Ecclesiastes, the most skeptical book of the bible, says more about the

---

[199] Ecclesiastes 2:13

enjoyment of life than any other.[200] Enjoyment is a gift from God and it is the way past cynicism.

Does that mean all enjoyment is healthy? Food is good. Too much food is not good. Accomplishment is good. Compulsive accomplishment comes with a price. There has never been an orgasm I did not enjoy, but some took more than they gave.

The relationship I had left my wife for was overwhelmed and finished after four years. I am grateful for the real support and companionship Mira offered in the most difficult time of my life, but after four years we were done.

My nineteen-year-old son gave me some great advice as I left: "Do something you really enjoy every day."

Some days it was coffee with friends. Other days it was going out to a movie. Then I moved to Italy. There I did something inspiring every day. I ate food and drank wine. I walked through history and contemplated great art. I signed up for tango lessons.

At my first full lesson the instructor informed me that his beautiful assistant would first teach me how to walk *con abbraccia*, with embrace. To lead in the tango a man must press the woman ahead. She must push back. It is the tension between the two that makes it all work. We were only half way around the room when my partner stopped, held me at arm's length, and said, "Stop leading with your hands and arms and start leading with your whole body." She was right. I lived from the shoulders up for most of my life, but that is not how life is enjoyed.

---

[200] Ecclesiastes 3:22; 5:19; 8:15; 9:9; 11:8

At the next lesson another woman began to dance with me. After one full turn she stopped me and said in the only words of English I ever heard from her, "You must be more sensual!"

You will not analyze your way out of cynicism. Enjoyment is the way. The sensual pleasures of good food, inspiring sounds and sights, measureable accomplishment, and warm sex will revive your life. Evangelicals have avoided true sensuality in their fear of sexual immorality. Ironically, that weakens rather than strengthens us.

Walking home one night to Michael and Rose's bed and breakfast I saw a marble plaque embedded in the wall of another house.

D.H.LAWRENCE
ENGLISH AUTHOR
11. 9. 1885 - 2. 3. 1930
LIVED HERE
1920 - 1923

D.H. Lawrence ended his novel *Lady Chatterley's Lover* with a scene that leaves readers wondering how the affair worked out. It's a good question. Affairs almost never work out. Then Lawrence wrote a thirty-seven page essay on sex, love, and the church[201]. There are a few bones in that fish that were hard to swallow but his argument for sensual passion that is of the body and not the mind is compelling. We need to feel passion rather than think about feeling it. The latter is a counterfeit. That's why masturbation hollows out the soul, Lawrence said. If D.H. Lawrence was right about the life of

---

[201] Lawrence, David, Herbert, Lady Chatterley's Lover, A Propos of "Lady Chatterley's Lover", Penguin Classics, 2006, p.235-272.

fantasy, pornography has taken an excavator to our souls. Porn is the junk-food of sex; tasty, but lacking nutrition. No matter how much you eat you are still empty. Men's minds race until their bodies no longer respond to real women unless surreal, remembered, or imagined images flash in their minds. Women have been catching up even if the fantasies are more focused emotionally. When we are artificial sexually, we become sexually cynical. The thoughtless pursuit of arousal trades intimacy for excitement and trust for thrills. The real goal is an integrity of action, thought, and feeling about sex. It requires honesty and practice. The outcome is intimacy, nourishment, and enjoyment. Trust for others is one reason to move beyond cynicism. Belief in our own strength and resilience is another reason.

Solomon set out to be wise, but found the task beyond his reach. So, he shifted his goal to discover the scheme of things and to understand "the stupidity of wickedness and the madness of folly."[202] In the very next verse Solomon says:

> I find more bitter than death
>   the woman who is a snare,
> whose heart is a trap
>   and whose hands are chains.
> The man who pleases God will escape her,
>   but the sinner she will ensnare.[203]

There is a kind of elusive woman who lures men in and reduces them to rabbits with snare-wire around their necks. Struggle tightens the noose. Her hands are warm weapons; a light touch on the arm, an understanding look, an

---

[202] Ecclesiastes 7:25b
[203] Ecclesiastes 7:26

affectionate hug. The cords of kindness are converted to chains. Once she has hold of you she will not let you go as long as you have something to give. One is always pursuing this woman but never catching her. How could a romance be more bitter than death? The loss of death is clear. Worse than that is a relationship that is always dying but never dead. Wisdom, pleasure, accomplishment, possessions, work or advancement can all ensnare us and leave us thinking that fulfillment lies in doing just a bit more.

Jesus said "everyone who sins is a slave to sin."[204] The Hebrews' slavery in Egypt is a potent image of that. Years after travelling to Egypt to escape the famine of their own land the descendants of Jacob became so prolific that their hosts feared and enslaved them. Slavery sometimes begins with the fulfillment of a real need. The Hebrews were forced to make the bricks that would build Egypt. Later, they were forced to gather the material for their work too. Later still they were told to kill their own male children. Slavery demands more and more while offering less and less. Eventually, we sacrifice our future.

What will please God and enable one to escape?

Try. Don't try too hard—every part of us needs to be ready to go—but try. Invite your friends to help you. I left Mira too many times to count. It was unfair to both of us. And even the last time I left I stood with my hands on my knees at the end of the driveway as dry heaves rolled through my body.

If the Hebrews in Egypt are a biblical metaphor for slavery to sin, the Exodus may be a parable of repentance, of the turn to freedom. After the initial euphoria of crossing the

---

[204] John 8:34

Red Sea out of Egypt, the Hebrews were thirsty and missed the flavors they had left behind. Leeks and garlic ran through their minds while they fled from those who killed their baby boys. The manna God provided was bland. I fasted once for forty days—what I missed most was flavor. Hunger, thirst, and grumbling about our empty spaces and unsatisfied appetites may be the natural path of repentance when we leave our sins behind. There was something that got us in to slavery. Why would we be surprised to miss it?

When relationships that started as something life-giving become a prison cell we're close to cynicism. The signs are a loss of hope and initiative. What was once inspiring isn't any more. When the trust is gone intimacy vanishes.

Solomon said that he couldn't find a woman he could trust anywhere and that a good man was almost impossible to find. I have heard women say the same thing about men. I may have been that kind of man. It's worse in romance than in other relationships because we hope for more. The opportunity for manipulation is huge.

My Dad taught me that unmet expectations are the source of all conflict. If someone has what we want but will not give it, there will be conflict. If we have the power to do what others want but will not, there will be conflict. When we want things from ourselves that we cannot deliver, there will be inner conflict. Expect disappointment. No one will give you everything you want. Almost everyone will disappoint you badly at some point. There is neither love nor life without pain.

If I could have done just one thing differently in my marriage, I would have had more fun with my wife. That's Solomon's advice: "Enjoy life with your wife."[205]

Enjoy things for what they are. That's the way out of cynicism.

There Is A Time For Everything.
> There is a time for everything,
> and a season for every activity under heaven:
> a time to be born and a time to die,
>   a time to plant and a time to uproot,
> a time to kill and a time to heal,
>   a time to tear down and a time to build,
> a time to weep and a time to laugh,
>   a time to mourn and a time to dance,
> a time to scatter stones and a time to gather them,
>   a time to embrace and a time to refrain,
> a time to search and a time to give up,
>   a time to keep and a time to throw away,
> a time to tear and a time to mend,
>   a time to be silent and a time to speak,
> a time to love and a time to hate,
>   a time for war and a time for peace.[206]

I sat in my study one Saturday evening and thought about the services I would preach in the next morning. It was the last church I pastored and a lot was going on. I thought about the strands of finance, staff, facilities, and programs, while Tchaikovsky's *Serenade for Strings* played in the background.

---
[205] Ecclesiastes 9:9
[206] Ecclesiastes 3:1-8

I imagined myself conducting an orchestra of people all expressing their skill and passion. Jesus came up to the podium and said, "Why don't you let me be the conductor and you play?." To live in time means letting God direct the tempo and dynamics for life. This means more than living by generalizations. It means watching and listening for the direction of the divine Spirit now.

There are signs that we are living out of time. These indicators live beyond the differences of temperament that bend one life one way and another a different way.

Lateness: People in other parts of the world are late because there is no hurry. In North America however, people are usually late because we are hurrying to get one more thing done.

Hurry: This is different than working quickly.

Strained expectations: Particularly with those we work with. When others are not keeping up it may be me who is living out of time. While it is an advantage to be faster than everyone else in a car race, in the everyday world it is a liability.

Glossy optimism: Like clothing worn shiny or threadbare by overuse, the smile that is forced, or the optimism that is pasted to our souls can be inappropriate in God's timing. Like a coin that only comes up heads, something seems wrong with it. Ironically, those who have been more involved with religion may have particular difficulty with this one-sidedness. After all, if the story is going to end well, it wouldn't seem quite right to grieve now, would it?

Persistent melancholy: If we never celebrate we're living out of time.

When we live only on one side of the coin or the other we understand neither time nor eternity for God "has made everything beautiful in its time. He has also set eternity in the hearts of men."[207] Eternity is a quality of life, not merely an endless measure of existence. Eternity is now. Do you know what time it is in your life? Where is the beauty? That's an indicator of how we should be living now.

In times of attraction and inspiration life is not a chore. "There is nothing better for men than to be happy and do good while they live."[208]

This does not mean that one always feels good, but that there is a rightness to things. Not only to love, but to hate. Not just to building, but to destruction. Laughter and mourning. Life and death. Conflict and peace.

When I volunteered on the Palliative Ward at Saint Paul's Hospital I watched people on the home stretch relinquish their lives. Peace is found in the release of things we were never meant to keep. Relinquishment isn't just letting go, it is entrusting the things we cannot hold on to, to one who can. This is manifested in practical ways, but it is an intensely spiritual exercise at the core.

In worship we find the opportunity to relinquish our egocentricity. In acknowledging another as Supreme, we relinquish our need to be alone at the center of the universe. Experience and intuition call for this. Maturity demands it.

In prayer, we relinquish control of our lives without abdicating responsibility. With the recognition that circumstances and the wills of others are out of our control, we are released from the manipulative spirit that sees others only for their value to our own purposes.

---

[207] Ecclesiastes 9:11
[208] Ecclesiastes 9:12

In petition, worry is relinquished and dependence takes its place. It is ironic that worry is always future in its orientation. No one ever worries about what has already happened. They worry about what might happen. While the healthy person may worry about the possibility of getting cancer, the cancer patient worries about the possibility of dying. Both worries are in the future and not worth carrying today.

Guilt is a crushing load. In isolation, it stoops lives and prevents people from moving on or up. Over many years I have listened to dying people tell their stories. Most of them, though not all, have told of some wrong they have committed or of how they have been wronged by another. The dying release things that have been locked away for years and kept even from close friends and family members. I have listened to the stories of the living too, and when they tell of the failures and frailties of their lives, freedom to live follows. In confession we relinquish failure—both our own and others. The freedom is palpable.

Finally, in prayer we relinquish self-reliance. The need for guidance that reaches beyond our vision, and strength beyond our own abilities releases us from self-imposed expectations that are false and delivers us from external dangers that are real.

My cancer surgeon was a considerate man. I discussed the possibility that I might somehow be healed before the time for my surgery came. In that hope, I asked the doctor to check one last time before he began cutting. It did not appear likely.

When the time for my surgery came the doctor met me in the pre-op room and made small talk for a moment before moving on to scrub. I followed shortly after him and found myself in the operating room with nurses and anaesthetists surrounding me. The gown was an ill fit and I felt vulnerable. Anaesthetic began to flow and my consciousness faded. Just then, in my last waking moment, the doctor reached over and lightly touched the lump on my neck, checking to see if it was still there.

It was a gentle gesture, and with it I relinquished my body to his care. I released my care to his will. It was no longer a choice I was forced into. He had my trust.

When we live in faith, there is a lighter touch to the timing and care of God.

The End Of The Matter

We know there is an accounting at some point,[209] but enjoy life while you can. To "be happy and do good…is the gift of God."[210]

Our family went to southern California a few months before I was diagnosed with cancer. I was weary. I took a nap in the afternoon and looked for reasons to go back to the hotel at night while my family was figuring how many rides could be ridden before they stopped running. My thoughts were fogged but I have good memories of riding small-time roller-coasters and of hurtling into plumes of spray while encased in a fiberglass log. My best memory is of walking back to the hotel with my six-year-old son. The rest were staying for the duration. As we came to the pirate ride he asked if we could go just once more.

There was no line and we sat at the very front. As we bobbed through the water to the first drop Aaron turned to me and said, "Put your hands up."

---

[209] Ecclesiastes 12:14
[210] Ecclesiastes 3:12,13

"What?" I asked.

"Put your hands up. It's more fun if you put your hands up and scream."

That is exactly what we did as we went over the first drop, and he was right. Life is better when you enjoy the ride.

9. Saved From Everything But Ourselves

A Messenger

My former wife listened to everything I said with little criticism in earlier days. She had something to say a few months after I left. "I am praying that God will send some messenger to you," she said. "Praying that like Balaam you will hear what God is saying."

Balaam was an Old Testament prophet headed for big trouble when his donkey finally spoke and told him to turn around because the angel of the Lord was on the path before them with his sword drawn to kill Balaam for his recklessness. Balaam had not been listening.[211]

I had not met Mira's brother in those days, but he called her sometimes when he got to drinking. He ran a crew of tree-planters who lived in the bush.

"My brother says he only knows two verses from the Bible," she relayed to me during one of those calls.

"What are they?" I asked and she passed the question back to him.

"Don't shit in the camp," was the first he said.[212] It was God's directions for the Children of Israel as they left Egypt and traveled through the desert to the Promised Land. A practical bit of advice for a community living in tents.

"A dog returns to its own vomit,"[213] was the second.

He discovered those scriptures while paging through purposely abandoned Bibles left by the evangelical students who worked for him each summer. I thought about those verses. I was too angry to read the Bible since being ejected

---
[211] Numbers 22
[212] Deuteronomy 23:12-14
[213] Proverbs 26:11

from the church. I couldn't separate the two. But I read those verses.

> For if God did not spare...the ancient world when he brought the flood on its ungodly people, but protected Noah, a preacher of righteousness, and seven others; if he condemned the cities of Sodom and Gomorrah by burning them to ashes, and made them an example of what is going to happen to the ungodly; and if he rescued Lot, a righteous man, who was distressed by the filthy lives of lawless men (for that righteous man, living among them day after day, was tormented in his righteous soul by the lawless deeds he saw and heard)— if this is so, then the Lord knows how to rescue godly men from trials and to hold the unrighteous for the day of judgment...
>
> With eyes full of adultery, they never stop sinning;... They have left the straight way and wandered off to follow the way of Balaam son of Beor, who loved the wages of wickedness. But he was rebuked for his wrongdoing by a donkey—a beast without speech—who spoke with a man's voice and restrained the prophet's madness.
>
> These men are springs without water and mists driven by a storm. Blackest darkness is reserved for them.... They promise them freedom, while they themselves are slaves of depravity—for a man is a slave to whatever has mastered him.... they are worse off at the end than they were at the

beginning... Of them the proverbs are true: 'A dog returns to its vomit'.[214]

I was scared. What if that was me? What if my adultery was driving me towards God's judgment? Mira and I had been openly together for several months.

The Friday after that phone call from her brother I had dinner waiting for Mira. When she drove up I put the salmon on the barbeque and set peppers and mushrooms around to roast. I didn't know how to deal with potential conflict with anything but niceness. We shared a glass of wine while we waited and then had another with dinner. After, she straddled me on the couch and asked, "What's wrong?"

"I've been thinking about what your brother said."

"About?"

"About those verses he knows. They are talking about me." I read them to her and she pulled back as I read.

"You think you're going to hell because of me?"

"Because of me," I said. I was the one who knew better. But she knew she was in that picture. "I have to end this," I said.

She ran downstairs and cursed as she kicked the wall.

"You let me drive all the way up here to break up with me?" she said. She had left her husband for me. Now this.

I waited. From the bottom of the stairs we began to talk again and then she came up. Part of me hoped she would know a way through this. Neither of us did. She cried, and yelled, and packed.

"Let me drive you back. I don't think you're in good shape to drive," I said.

---

[214] 2 Peter 2:3-22

"I don't want to be in the same car as you. You make dinner for me and give me wine. Were you going to make love with me too before you broke up with me?"

Forty-five minutes after she left I started my van and followed until I saw that she was safe in her driveway.

On the way home it dawned on me that whatever God rescued Noah and Lot from, it wasn't bad behavior. Noah disembarked the ark, planted a vineyard and got drunk. His son saw him naked and Noah cursed him.[215] Lot left a town where the men were ready to bang down his door to get a crack at his guests, but Lot ended up in a cave so drunk that he slept with his two daughters and they both got pregnant.[216] It seems that while God saved those righteous men from His judgment, He didn't save them from themselves.

Repentance

For five years after I had an affair people urged me to repent. The word repentance means "to turn". People meant that I should turn away from my sin. I listened and even applied their suggestions. I tried prayer counseling and psychotherapy. I wept on my face for days at a time and "just did it." I returned to my wife as an act of faith in the hope that God would give me the strength of heart to continue. None of these acts produced the expected results.

In hindsight, my reasons for repentance had little to do with God. I felt guilt, shame and fear. My focus was on my moral failure. I had something to turn from, but I needed something to turn to.

There is a serpentine curve just north of the American border on 8th Avenue that curls up through a ravine east of

---

[215] Genesis 9:20-25
[216] Genesis 19:30-38

192nd Street. It is the best set of corners for ten kilometers in any direction and I almost hurt myself there.

I was on a sportbike with the power, brakes and a riding position that begged you to find corners. Brake. Lean. Accelerate. Straighten. Again.

It was my third time through. Faster than the second, which had been quicker than the first. Coming into the third bend I looked at the gravel shoulder before the bank dropped into the ravine. I was going too fast to make the corner if I rolled onto the loose rock, but I was headed there. My focus made my fear a reality. I took my inside foot off the peg and the bike fish-tailed in the dirt. I slid right to the edge before I regained control.

You cannot turn by looking where you do not want to go.

I went back and rode the set of curves again. This time I looked up through the corner to where I wanted to go. I rolled the throttle off, squeezed the brake and leaned into the turn before rolling the gas on again at the apex. The bike righted itself as I exited the corner.

It is almost impossible to turn your life when you are looking at where you don't want to be. A hopeless man does not repent. Our lives turn in repentance when we look ahead to the good. Jesus said "Repent, for the kingdom of heaven has come near."[217]

When I asked those who told me to repent, "How?", at some point the answers I got were things I had already tried. I was frustrated. Who could I ask? I didn't know anyone who had been through things just as I had. I reasoned the bible

---

[217] Matthew 4:17

might have the answer and I had the skills and motivation to dig it out given time.

I studied every reference to repentance in the Scripture and studied the historical use of the word too. I contemplated the stories of all those whose lives had turned. In the end, I found, if not a guarantee, then guidance. I learned that while we can turn away from our sins, only God can turn us to life. Repentance in the Scripture is in response to an encounter with God, and it is God who chooses when he will show up. No one in the bible repents until God shows up in word, in deed or in person. Whether it is in the burning bush with Moses after forty years, or on the seashore with Peter after forty days, that is when the life-giving fullness of repentance arrives.

The reason for repentance is not so much because we are bad, but because the kingdom of God is so good! Repentance and the kingdom of heaven are linked because both are defined by the presence of God. The kingdom of God and the experiential knowledge of God are interchangeable.[218] Repentance is not so much judicial as it is relational; it's less about rules and more about love, less of a command and more of an invitation. The call to repentance is not a burden, it is good news! Here's why. The kingdom of heaven is about healing, freedom, and growth.

The Kingdom Of Heaven Is About Healing, Freedom And Growth

> Jesus went throughout Galilee, teaching in their synagogues, proclaiming the good news of

---

[218] Kingdom (Matthew 23:13) and experiential knowledge (*gnosis*, Luke 11:52) are used interchangeably.

the kingdom, and healing every disease and sickness among the people.[219]

Words were not enough. Jesus restored lepers and healed paralytics. He stopped the hemorrhaging of women and opened the ears and mouths of deaf mutes. Jesus gave sight to the blind. When Jesus sent his disciples out to proclaim the good news of the kingdom he told them to heal the sick.[220]

My friend Lara did not conceive easily and had miscarried repeatedly. She wanted another child but was afraid to try again. Each loss hurt too much.

"I believe God has another child for you," I said.

After prayer, Lara got pregnant and kept the child until a lively baby was born. Three weeks later Lara came to me with the baby in her arms. The child was listless and Lara cried.

"There's a hematoma," Lara said and pointed to the baby's head. There was visible swelling and a cat-scan had showed a pocket of blood big enough to fill a woman's hand. It was not diminishing with time. I took the infant, walked to the corner of the sanctuary and held her tight in my arms. The Spirit was there that day with power to heal and I hugged that baby close and prayed fervently and with faith for her healing.

The next day no swelling was visible. A new scan showed the hematoma was gone.

"I don't believe in God," the doctor said as she cried. "But this doesn't happen." The kingdom of heaven brings healing to those who have broken.

The kingdom of God brings freedom. When Jesus crossed over from Galilee to the Gentile region of the

---

[219] Matthew 4:23
[220] Luke 9:1,2

177

Gerasenes, a demon-possessed man met him.[221] In the man's torment he had stopped wearing clothes and abandoned his home for a solitary life among the tombs. Others tried to restrain his madness but when the demon seized him even chains could not hold him. There are inner problems whose solution is beyond external controls.

Jesus asked him, "What is your name?"[222]

When we are assaulted by motivations and voices beyond our control God asks, *Who are you?* How long had it been since anyone wanted to know, not how to control him, but who he was? It was not the man who answered, but the demon.

"Legion," he replied, because many demons had gone into him.[223]

I have encountered people so overcome that they lost their voice. Their identity was submerged. Whether through the wounds of abuse, the bitterness of unforgiveness, or persistence in what was known to be hurtful and wrong, doors were opened to destructive, deceptive and accusing spiritual forces.

Jesus commanded the impure spirits to come out of the man and they fled into a herd of pigs that ran into the sea and drowned! When the people of the region came to see what had happened they found the man sitting at Jesus' feet, clothed and in his right mind. Those people were terrified and asked Jesus to leave. I wonder why? Did change terrify them? Was there something they had done to that man?

When I was thirty and working on my Master's Degree in spirituality I went on an outreach mission to the city of

---
[221] Luke 8:26-33
[222] Luke 8:30
[223] Luke 8:30b

Penticton. A desperate woman had called the ministers of the city for help; she had lost almost all control. I had fasted and prayed before the mission from my own sense of need. A supportive group gathered around the woman, affirmed her, and drove out the demons that falsely accused her and undermined her identity and value. Not every voice in our heads is our own. The woman in Penticton went from rolling on the floor, growling and speaking in other voices, to sitting and conversing in her right mind. She wrote a year later to say she was well.

One of those nights in Penticton I went to an outreach event that no one came to. The hostess had invited her friends and colleagues and made lasagna for twenty. While we waited for those who never came we talked about our families.

Without thinking I turned to her and said, "You need to forgive your brother." *Why did I say that?* I thought!

I didn't even know if she had a brother. The hostess began to cry. Years before her brother had held a knife to her throat and threatened to kill her. Fear and resentment had overshadowed her since then. In a simple prayer she told God of her forgiveness for her brother and asked for freedom from fear. Our demons take different forms; some are physically debilitating, others are like echoes from the past that leave us no peace.

How many more people would want to enter the divine kingdom if they were healed from what hindered, and freed from what haunted them? That's how our lives begin turning in repentance. The kingdom of heaven begins with a turn to health and freedom, and it grows from there.

Without ever saying exactly what the kingdom is, Jesus spoke about the kingdom all the time. The kingdom of God is not something I preached about. I checked. In my last fifteen years as a preacher I never spoke once about the kingdom of God. When Jesus' forerunner John the Baptizer was thrown in prison and stopped from preaching, Jesus started with the same message. "Repent, for the kingdom of heaven has come near."[224]

When Jesus sent his disciples out to preach, he sent them out to proclaim the good news of the kingdom.[225] The kingdom of God (or of heaven; rarely of Christ or of light), is mentioned one hundred and seven times in the Gospels. The church is mentioned three times on just two occasions, and only in Matthew.[226] I had that backwards. When Jesus rose from the dead he appeared to his disciples and "spoke about the kingdom of God."[227] The disciples asked if he was going to restore the power to Israel. It is some consolation that those who spent three years with Jesus didn't understand the kingdom of God either. They began to live it when they were unmistakably filled with the divine Spirit.[228]

Jesus spoke often about what the kingdom of heaven is *like*. The kingdom of God is like a farmer sowing good seed; soil conditions affect its growth and there are inevitably weeds.[229] The kingdom is like a mustard seed, or like yeast; it starts small but grows out of all proportion.[230] The kingdom of heaven is like hidden treasure or a spectacular pearl; it is worth everything one has.[231] The kingdom is like a fishing net that

---

[224] Matthew 3:2; 4:17
[225] Matthew 10:7; Luke 9:2; 10:9
[226] Once, when Peter recognizes Jesus' divine identity and mission, Jesus says he will build his church(Matthew 16:18). Oddly, Peter makes no use of the word church (*ecclesia*) in his letters. The word church, is thoroughly secular, a gathering. Why did Jesus and the early Christians use a secular instead of religious term?
[227] Acts 1:3
[228] Acts 2ff
[229] Matthew 13:1-9, 18-30
[230] Matthew 13:31-33
[231] Matthew 13:44-46

gathers people in; the angels separate the catch at the end of the age.[232] It is like a wedding celebration that you don't want to miss.[233] The kingdom of heaven is about stewardship.[234]

Evangelicals commonly use the word stewardship to mean fund-raising, usually in reference to building programs. Stewardship means something more in the bible. Stewardship is making more of what we've been given. Stewardship is what an Italian carpenter named Giuseppe taught me when I was just thirteen. He trained me to add value to materials with creativity, work and skill until I could build a house by the time I finished high school. Giuseppe taught me to watch what he was doing and then he watched as I tried. As his apprentice and helper he taught me to think ahead about what was needed next. In the kingdom of God, what is the divine doing and how can I move and work with that? How can I make the most of my experience, gifts, passion and resources? That is stewardship.

Jesus was on his way to Jerusalem and everyone thought the kingdom was going to be established immediately so Jesus told a parable.[235]

A man of substance was going away and before he left he gave several of his servants some money to oversee. When the man returned some of the servants had doubled the money entrusted to them! One of the servants however, was afraid of the risks and knew his master was a demanding man, so he buried the money. When the master returned he commended the stewards who had made more of what was

---

[232] Matthew 13:47-50
[233] Matthew 22:1-14; 25:1-13
[234] Matthew 25:14-30
[235] Luke 19:11-27; also Matthew 25:14-30

given them. But he chastised the fearful steward, took what he had, and gave it to one who would make better use of it.

Most of us fall somewhere below the last steward in Jesus parable. If God was to ask what we have done with the resources entrusted to our care, many of us would have to respond: "I spent it." We have stooped below the level of the worst steward. We are consumers.

Consumerism is killing us, and the earth. After a century of economic growth and material prosperity, the west is in trouble. Our focus on creating wealth has damaged our most precious assets; our bodies and the planet we live on. Obesity and diabetes are epidemic. Inactivity and poor diet are undermining our health and strength. Our relentless hunger for products is consuming the world's resources and corrupting the environment. Our appetite for fossil fuels is polluting the earth, and unchecked, will make the world uninhabitable. It is not enough to be well-motivated. Jesus commended a steward who was shady but shrewd.[236] The focus on accumulation has prevented us from another aspect of stewardship; caring for each other. A good servant in the kingdom is one who takes care of others.[237] The growing disparity of rich and poor testifies against us.

What if God showed up now and asked how we have stewarded the treasures of our bodies, our planet and those in our care? He would reward us like the last steward: "throw that worthless servant outside."[238]

Stewardship is what an old cowboy taught me as a boy when he showed me how to live in the bush. "You always leave things as good or better than you found them."

---

[236] Luke 16:1-9
[237] Matthew 24:45-51
[238] Matthew 25:30

The kingdom of heaven is the kingdom of glory.[239] Steinbeck caught the scent of glory in East of Eden:

> Sometimes a kind of glory lights up the mind of a man. It happens to nearly everyone. You can feel it growing or preparing like a fuse burning toward dynamite…. A man may have lived all of his life in the gray, and the land and trees of him dark and somber. The events, the important ones, may have trooped by faceless and pale. And then—the glory—so that a cricket song sweetens his ears, the smell of the earth rises chanting to his nose, and dappling light under a tree blesses his eyes. Then a man pours outward, a torrent of him, and yet he is not diminished. And I guess a man's importance in the world can be measured by the quantity and number of his glories.[240]

Glory is the nature of God. It is the nature of God's kingdom too. It is what humanity hungers for.

A Kingdom Without Condemnation

The kingdom of heaven is a kingdom without condemnation. Prostitutes and corrupt bureaucrats are welcome. The poor and hungry have special rewards in the kingdom. It is hard for the rich to enter the kingdom and impossible for the arrogant. Those who sneak in thinking their good works have entitled their entry will be cast out. The kingdom is not about outward observances.

---

[239] Kingdom and glory are interchangeable in Matthew 20:21 and Mark 10:37.
[240] Steinbeck, John, East of Eden, Penguin Books, p.130

I volunteered on the palliative ward for AIDS and cancer patients at St. Paul's Hospital every Thursday afternoon for several years after I myself had cancer. There was a lot of judgment talk about homosexuals and AIDS in the churches in those days and I felt I should be talking less about loving "sinners" and doing it more. No one on the ward knew I was a minister for the first year and a half.

Across from the nursing station and in bed four was the man who had lived longer in those days than anyone else in Vancouver with AIDS.[241]

"So you're a minister?"

"I am, but that's not why I'm here."

"Why are you here?"

"Here to listen. Here to do something that doesn't have anything to do with being a minister."

"Do you think God sends homosexuals to hell?" the patient asked.

"I think God could find good reasons to send every one of us to hell if that was what he wanted."

"I guess we can talk."

That man told me of the loss of almost all his friends, of four, or five, or six funerals in one month; of the early days of AIDS in Vancouver.

"We would hook up with someone at the bar, be gone for an hour and go back to find someone else. Sometimes four or five." He paused, and added, "It was crazy."

"Do you have regrets?"

"Not for what I did. But I wish I had understood the deep kind of love that keeps you with one person sooner."

"Did you find that?"

---

[241] I have altered the details of this encounter to protect people's identities.

"I did... He died."

I doubt that God condemns people to hell for their orientation. I have a gay son and I would not. Sodom was a city where men were ready to tear down doors and break into people's houses to rape someone new to town.[242] It wasn't the first time something like that happened in Sodom. The Bible says there was a great outcry against the city.[243] In Isaiah's writing God compares Israel to Sodom; a place of injustice and violence.[244] The prophet Ezekiel said the sin of Sodom was being "arrogant, overfed and unconcerned; they did not help the poor and needy."[245] Again in Ezekiel God says the wanton immorality of Israel is worse than that of Sodom and the reference is not to orientation but to the perverse selfishness of it.[246]

The book of Leviticus does say that homosexuality is an abomination. It also says that shellfish are an abomination and not to be eaten and that anyone having sex with a woman during her period is to be cut off from the community. Adulterers are to be killed. Jesus said Capernaum was worse than Sodom and that Sodom would have turned around if they had experienced the miracles Jesus performed in Capernaum.[247] Does anyone really think it would be more acceptable to God if all the heterosexual men in a city banged on someone's door and threatened to kill a family if they didn't turn over their two female houseguests? God is less

---

[242] Genesis 18:1-5, 16-33; 19:1-29
[243] Genesis 18:20
[244] Isaiah 1
[245] Ezekiel 16:49
[246] Ezekiel 16
[247] Matthew 11:23

interested in our orientation than he is in the quality of our relationships and commitments.

The kingdom of heaven is not defined by ethics, but by desire and direction. Keep asking. Continue to seek. Don't stop knocking on God's door.[248] The kingdom of God is received as a gift,[249] yet it takes all you have to be in the kingdom. It is not about knowledge, but it is about knowing God. The kingdom of God is not merely about satisfying our appetites, but it is about the fulfillment of righteousness, peace and joy.[250] One enters the kingdom through a rebirth that is conceived by God. The first breath of this kingdom life is from the divine Spirit. It is received like a child and embraced by faith.[251]

I had moved out from Mira and lived alone for nine months when it was time for my last eye operation. My son stayed the night and would take me to the hospital and back. Our alarms went off at the same time.

I stood in the bathroom and put steroid drops in my eye. I could read the label if I held it five inches from my face. Everything beyond that was blurred.

My son made chocolate milk in the kitchen, the same thing he had every morning when I lived with his mother. The clink of the spoon in the glass was familiar.

At the hospital I waited on a gurney and listened to a woman on the intercom reading from the bible. The noise of the pre-op room overshadowed the words until the voice began to pray.

---

[248] Mathew 5:19,20
[249] Luke 12:32
[250] Romans 14:17
[251] John 3:5-17

"Our Father…"

A nurse came and told me my lens implant had not yet arrived.

"Thy Kingdom come…"

I moved to another bed.

"Thy will be done…"

When the surgeon was done he taped a patch over my right eye. My son appeared and led me home. I walked to my bedroom and set my glasses on the dresser. I had worn corrective lenses since I was eleven.

The next morning I rose from my bed, pulled the quilt taught, turned the sheet down and placed the pillows. My glasses stayed on the dresser. The linoleum on my bathroom floor was cool under my bare feet as I flicked the light switch and stood for a moment. Turning to the mirror my index nail picked at the flush edge of the medical tape on my forehead. My fingers pulled down and peeled away the shield that had guarded my right eye through the night.

Clarity.

"Where did all those wrinkles come from?" I whispered.

When I laughed at my reflection the creases danced. My eyes glimmered back at me in the glass on the bathroom wall.

I went to the window and opened the blinds. The sky hinted at royal blue over English Bay and lightened to a pastel where a few clouds wisped over the snow-dusted peaks above Howe Sound. The trees that undulate between the seawall and Beach Avenue were turning through umber and ochre as they wound toward the park. I could see the leaves on trees! I could see ski runs slashing through the forest on Cypress Mountain.

Individual trees poked up from the crest like teeth on a comb. To the north I made out the rifts and rills that intersect the summits of the Lions and the dusting of snow on those peaks was icing on my cake.

A swarm of black dots swept up from the right and my heart paused. I saw dots like that four years before when my left retina first detached; black dots that hovered and darted like flies. That was eight operations ago. I saw them again when my right retina detached. But this day it was a flock of birds and as they flew up and towards me their dark wings glinted with crisp light from the east. All this I saw with clarity.

This is what I see clearly:

Life is messy. No one gets through life without heartbreak and entanglement.

God is compassionate. He looks beyond our faults and meets our need.

God is with us.

Not in the pristine places where we overcoat our flaws, but wherever there is an authentic heart. That is why Jesus was begotten in this world. God is with us.

The Kingdom Of Heaven Is Near

Noah and Lot are paired together in the words of Jesus too.[252] The Pharisees, the religious elite of the day, asked Jesus when the kingdom of God would come. Everyone was waiting for God to show up and overthrow their political oppressors and give them temporal power instead. Jesus said the kingdom of God is not here or there, it is not about

---

[252] Luke 17:20-28

external observance, "because the kingdom of God is within you."[253]

The people who asked about the kingdom were not Jesus' disciples, they were his enemies, looking for a way to discredit him and eventually kill him. Could I say that to my adversaries? Could I look into the eyes of the ones who tripped me up and blocked my best efforts in what I believed was God's will and say: *The divine kingdom is near you, it's in your midst, it is within you!*

It is a question of desire.

"Who is it you want?"[254] On the last night of his life Jesus asked that twice when the soldiers and religious officials came to take him. When the divine asks a question it's important. When the same question is asked twice we should look for the answer. *Who is it you want?*

Judas sealed things with a kiss. Peter took out a sword and struck the high priest's servant and cut off his right ear. Jesus told him to put it away. The kingdom of God is not about that kind of power. Jesus was bound and led away to the high priest and then to the Roman governor Pilate.

'Are you the king of the Jews?'[255] Pilate asked.

Jesus said, 'My kingdom is not of this world. If it were, my servants would fight to prevent my arrest by the Jewish leaders. [Isn't that what Peter had just done?] But now my kingdom is from another place… In fact, the reason I was born and came into the world is to

---

[253] Luke 17:20,21 KJV
[254] John 18:4,7
[255] John 18:33

testify to the truth. Everyone on the side of truth listens to me.'

'What is truth?' retorted Pilate.[256]

"Who is it you want?" is the answer.

Jesus is the truth;[257] the living, personal, divine, human truth. Entering the kingdom of God isn't about how much you know or even what you've done. Some who have delivered God's messages, who have driven out demons and performed miracles, will not enter the kingdom of heaven.[258]

The point of Jesus' Sermon on the Mount is not about *what we do* to enter the kingdom of God. The moral standard is impossible. After setting the bar above adultery to purity of thought,[259] above murder to a life free of proud anger,[260] Jesus said,

"Keep asking and it will be given to you. Keep seeking and you will find. Keep knocking and the door will be opened to you."[261]

The kingdom lives in those who know they are not all that, in those who are hungry. It is not about technique, but desire. Seek first the kingdom of God.

Six years after leaving the church I cleared departures at Leonardo da Vinci Airport in Rome.

"Do you have a map?" I asked the smiling woman at the information desk.

---

[256] John 18:36-38
[257] John 14:6
[258] Matthew 7:21-23
[259] Matthew 5:27-30
[260] Matthew 5:21,22
[261] Matthew 7:7,8 author's paraphrase

"You want a treasure map?" she replied and sent me on my way.

I fell asleep on the train and when I woke twenty minutes later an ancient Roman tower stood just outside the window. Ahead was Termini Station, the end of the line.

The apartment where I would stay was only three blocks away. I was drawn to the large lobby, the dark wood and the steps worn smooth from many ascents. After dinner with wine in a goblet the size of a bowl, I closed the shutters, drank lots of water and brushed my teeth and tongue, stacked two pillows and fell asleep.

That night I dreamed a lucid dream; I was asleep yet conscious. In my dream I balanced in a horizontal yoga pose with my hands beneath me on the rock-solid floor. My head tilted down and my feet angled up—and then—*bliss*.

Not a dream about enlightenment, but knowledge, not an idea of ecstasy, but unbounded joy. It was not an explanation, but an experience, and how does one describe such a thing? Like offering a menu it gives an idea, but a menu is not a meal, nor is it flavor or nourishment. In that eternal moment I knew, and I was known. The universe encompassed me in constellations of space and knowledge and emotion. I was conscious of everything and distracted by nothing, and I was lucid in that ecstasy. *If I could live in this I wouldn't even miss sex,* I thought. I knew my conscious mind had, and probably would again, cover up this awareness, but it is within. Time and place were within. I encountered the God who lives within, and within whom everything lives.

What if God really is omnipresent? Not as an idea, but in every bit of reality that surrounds and fills us. What if we really do live and move and have our being in the divine? Not just in some mystical sense, but practically, naturally, and spiritually?

God is everywhere. The omnipresence of God was taught in sermons and theology classes but I never considered the practical reality that God is in everything. He is in every molecule of the desk I made from planks of black walnut and am writing on. He is in every leaf of the trees across the street, and in every breath that we breathe. Evangelical fear of Pantheism, the belief that everything is God, held us back from experiencing the God who is in everything; held us on the beach by the ocean of God's presence. In God "we live and move and have our being."[262] The divine image is encoded in every bit of us.

When the Pharisees tried to trip Jesus up and asked if taxes should be paid to the Romans, Jesus asked for a coin.[263] They thought they had him. If Jesus said yes, the people would reject him. If he said no, the Romans would arrest him. Someone produced a coin and Jesus asked whose image was on it. "Caesar's," was the reply. Jesus said "So give back to Caesar what is Caesar's, and to God what is God's."[264] We were created in, and live with, the divine image.[265]

"Start seeing everything as God," the happily inspiring poet Hafiz said. "But keep it a secret."[266] The kingdom of God is that near.

A Kingdom Of Compassion

Four years after leaving Mona I woke laying on my back and thought *How did I get here?* I could not feel my hands.

---

[262] Acts 17:28
[263] Matthew 22:15-22
[264] Matthew 22:21
[265] Genesis 1:27
[266] Hafiz, Trans. By Daniel Ladinsky, I Heard God Laughing, Penguin Books, p.58

I raised them and then traced the horizontal scar on my neck from my thyroidectomy. My mouth was swollen and I spoke with a lisp. My palate had been peeled back to remove a tumor between the roots of my front teeth a week before. My ears buzzed all the time. My vision was blurred and out of alignment from the many operations. *I have lost my senses*, I thought.

There is a bible story of a son who lost his senses.[267] He told his father he wanted his inheritance early, the middle-eastern equivalent of saying *I wish you were already dead*. The son's lack of restraint didn't end there, and before long he had moved away and dissipated everything on parties and easy friends. Once everything, including his stomach, was empty, he thought of his father again. His father's servants did better than he was doing. The son was feeding pigs and hoping for a stray corn husk.

The young man relinquished his claims and headed home hoping for work. The father saw him coming. Fresh clothes. A big hug. A feast. The son didn't see that coming. Of course he didn't have it coming, but that's grace. Grace doesn't make sense, but we all hope to see it, to hear a word of welcome, to smell and taste the good things we squandered, to feel a warm touch, to live with the sense of what is good again. Amazingly, God often draws us to himself with kindness. The prodigal son returned not from fear but in the hope of the father's goodness.

As I am writing this I call my parents and ask if they remember the day I told them of my affair.

---

[267] Luke 15:11-32

"We were heartbroken," my mother says. "You were broken and we were afraid for your life. I used to believe in compassion," Mom said, "but now I am living it."

My dad says he read Romans chapter two that day. "Who were we to despise the kindness of God that leads to repentance," he paraphrases. "What you needed was kindness."

Some translations of the ancient story of the lost son say the prodigal came to his senses; the first version says literally that "he came to himself." If he did, he came to more of himself than he had ever been. The sense of entitlement was gone, replaced with an honest hope. Not the guaranteed kind of hope that the moralists preach when they say that if you do this, you will certainly get that. The prodigal son took hope in his father's goodness without demanding it. He knew too that if he did not do something, things would not get better. After losing all he had, the lost son found himself. He was saved from everything but himself. That is what happens in the kingdom of heaven; compassion brings us to God and to ourselves. The kingdom of heaven is that near.

10. End With Hope

The path to hope is grief.

I have a friend who contributed generously financially but seldom came to my church. When he did come he could be counted on for crisp criticism—unsuitable ushers, the appearance of a certain musician, that sort of thing. At the end of one particular service he lingered at the back and gave me the best preaching advice I ever received. "Always end with hope."

We need that; we need to know and feel that things will turn out well, that we and those we love will be okay. Life teaches a different lesson.

Health fails, love falters, friends hurt us and we ourselves fall below the line of our own expectations. Worse yet, God does not play by his own rules. In the Bible he sends deceiving prophets, arbitrarily hardens one heart and softens another, wipes out whole cities and yet says he does not want anyone to perish.[268] Hope is not predictable.

In what may be the oldest book of the bible, a man named Job lost everything, and found hope. It began with a contest in heaven.

One day after roaming back and forth over the earth Satan[269] presented himself before God.[270]

"Did you take a look at my man Job?" God asked. "He's flawless!"[271]

---

[268] 1 Kings 22:1-28; Joshua 11:20, Romans 9:18; Joshua 6:21, Joshua 10:40-42; 2 Peter 3:9
[269] Satan was an angel who had been thrown out of heaven for pride. Satan means adversary.
[270] Job 1:6-12

Indeed, Job's life was perfect. Even the numbers used to describe his family and livestock are metaphors for perfection. He was pious and humble and recognized as the greatest of men.

"Of course he's a good man," Satan said, "You've given him nothing but good. Take away all he has and he'll curse you to your face."[272]

In one day Job lost it all; thieves stole his oxen (the means of cultivation), fire fell from heaven and consumed his sheep (the means of sustenance and clothing), more thieves stole his camels (the means of transportation), and finally, a great wind blew the house down and all his children were killed (the way we live beyond ourselves).

"Naked I came from my mother's womb,
and naked I will depart." Job said.
"The LORD gave and the LORD has taken away;
may the name of the LORD be praised."[273]

The adversary came back and God rubbed it in. "Even though you gave him a reason to hate me, he doesn't"![274]

"Skin for skin!" Satan replied. "A man will give all he has for his own life. But now stretch out your hand and strike his flesh and bones, and he will surely curse you to your face."[275]

So, Job was struck with painful sores that covered his entire body and he scraped at his pain with a shard of broken

---

[271] Job 1:8 author's paraphrase
[272] Job 1:9 a.p.
[273] Job 1:21
[274] Job 2:1-6 a.p.
[275] Job 2:4

pottery while he sat in the ashes of his life. Hope doesn't mean we don't go through it. It doesn't mean we don't feel it either.

The conventional wisdom on hope, both then and now, says that if you do everything right, everything will be all right. Our hope is in our own hands. Keep the rules, be patient, and good will come. God doesn't live in that box.

A Truer Hope

After years of determined optimism I lost myself and my hope at about the same time. My belief in the innate goodness of humanity bled into the red soil of Rwanda. I lost my belief in organized religion when religious leaders assured me they were working for my good while doing the opposite behind my back. I don't believe in marriage as a principle, though if I met someone who was all that, I would give myself entirely to them. I have painfully relinquished the ideal of love, but there are those I love and who I know love me. I lost hope before all of this, and I do not believe in hope now, but I believe in God and I believe in myself and somehow I am a man of faith.

There is no hope without faith. Unless we believe in God and in ourselves even as God does, fear will be our habitude. In that relationship of trust, we are to live with hope not just in difficulty, but even when times are good.

When my hopes and trusts were stripped away I lost all my convictions except the belief that God was with me, and that even if I was faithless (and I was) he himself would be faithful.[276] New convictions slowly grew like sprouts from the ashes of the field I burned as a little boy. I had been playing with matches.

---

[276] 2 Timothy 2:13

The first step was honesty. A day came when I realized I couldn't leave my lover and return and stay with my wife. What I could do was tell the truth. I stopped telling people what they wanted to hear and started telling the messy and uncomfortable truth about myself. Honesty was the most significant choice in my journey through an affair. Job wasn't just honest about himself, he spoke frankly and truthfully about what God was doing with him.[277]

I am not Job. I have hurt some more deeply than others hurt me. If Job was blameless, I wasn't. But, like Job, neither did I curse God. How different would all of our relationships be if we could bring all of our intensity and sadness and anger and grief into the relationship instead of allowing it to propel us away?

The Path To Hope Is Grief

After listening to a hundred stories of horror and trying to persuade Rwandan pastors to open themselves and trust one another just a bit, I caught a cab back to the monastery at the edge of Butare. To the right of the long driveway and down the grassy hill women were meeting. Around the field where they sat were many mounds. The Rwandans wore brightly dyed dresses or skirts that wrapped around them in sharp contrast to their dark features. Smiles and laughter rolled up the hill. I walked down.

Music began to play. Women circled and clapped and swayed. On the edge of the circle a tall slender woman smiled and said hello. There was an indentation in her forehead almost an inch deep and the size of a dollar coin over her right eye. The skin had healed in the shape of her wound. Tragedy

---

[277] Job 42:7,8

had banished awkwardness and I asked for her story. Her husband had been killed first and then her children. She had been raped. The empty space in her head was where she had been hit with a hammer and left for dead.

She began to smile again. "Would you like to dance?"

She found a different hope, I thought.

The path to hope is grief. Like coal converted to diamonds, it doesn't come easily. You won't find a hope that lives beyond circumstances without going through grief. A truer hope is not about what we expect from life.

While I was in the thick of being a pastor, I sat beside my friend Erik in a hospital corridor. Those were the days before his wife Lara's healing and she was having an ultrasound to determine if the child within her was still alive. A nurse rolled her gurney out of the examination room and down the hall toward us. Tears streaked Lara's face. Her hands rested on her belly and clutched a small vial containing the tiny lifeless form. The child had died. When something we care about is beyond our reach, yet still so near that it hurts, that is grief.

On the seventh anniversary of the genocide in Rwanda I spent every afternoon for a week listening to university students in Kigali tell of their losses. At the end of the first day I was told that many would not be able to come the next day. There was a funeral for a friend.

"What happens when someone dies in Rwanda?" I asked.

"The first night, all the friends and relatives come to the family's home. They bring food and they might light a fire so everyone can sit around and be with the family. Usually the person is buried the next day."

I asked if that finished things and another student told me that friends continue to gather every night for a week.

"What do they do?"

"We tell the stories of the person's life."

Since going to Rwanda I had heard only the stories of people's deaths. Machetes, machine guns, grenades, rocket launchers. No one had told me the stories of their loved one's lives. I had heard the horrors; I had not shared the goodness of the lives that are gone.

"Were there funerals for those who were killed?"

"Not many. What could we bury?"

We don't process our grief by asking why, but by remembering the good that has been lost.

Job's three friends gathered around his grief and for a week they sat without a word.

"What I feared has come upon me,"[278] Job said.

Why is anyone surprised when God takes us through our fears? Kierkegaard said God blesses those he curses and curses those he blesses. Fear is the opposite of hope and the path to hope goes through our fears. We are delivered to our fears and from optimism before we find true hope. Fears can be skirted, but it only prolongs things.

What am I afraid of?

In the bible, hope is the opposite of fear.

It is easy to talk from a distance about the benefits of suffering. But up close, fingers clench, backs arc and throats tighten to hold in the scream. Where did we get the idea that faith and hope would remove the pain? Hope is not an anaesthetic, but it enables us to endure. There is deep hurt

---

[278] Job 3:25

before deep hope. Suffering now is part of joy later. We don't get that then without this now. Like my scarred cornea that was cut out and replaced with a new one that took months and months to heal, my new hopes took time to quiet.

Job's comforters reasoned that Job must have done something really wrong. There had to be a reason for his disaster. Job's three friends were the conventional voice of wisdom. They saw things in terms of cause and effect. Do this, get that. False hope counts on controllable factors. True hope connects with the One who cannot be controlled. Taking hope exclusively into one's own hands creates entitlement or insecurity. If God rewards the hope of those who are good, how good does one have to be? That's what bothered Job most; it was all so unjust.[279]

Mira and I were at a wilderness campsite when I saw a minister I knew in the site behind us.

"Would you tell me what happened?" he asked.

I told him of my burnout, of abandonment and betrayal by friends, of spiritual leaders who said one thing while they did another.

"That happens when we stray from God's will," he commented.

"That happened before my moral failure," I said.

"I hadn't heard it that way," he finished, but he didn't pull away.

If my sins were worse than Job's, my friends were better. After living in a community of hundreds, there were only a handful left. Some called every day when I was at my

---

[279] Job 31:1-40

worst and took me for lunch as my mind struggled to make sense of the senseless. I could call any time. Later, my friend Martin told me God had told him to simply be my friend. *Don't tell him what to do.* Martin is a prominent minister and it is hard for healers to be with the un-fixable. When he was especially tempted to speak, he bit his cheek.

"Sometimes I bled," he told me later.

Stages Of Grief

I was twenty and nailing the last few boards on the roof of an apartment I was building when a passerby told me the first floor was on fire.

"How bad?" I asked.

"Pretty bad" he said.

A smoldering bit of wood behind pipes the plumbers soldered had burst into flame. I ran downstairs and crab-walked under the flames to get at the source of the fire. The extinguisher emptied with the end of the flames.

The reconstruction proceeded in stages. Bit by bit I cut, removed and replaced one charred section after another. If I had done it all at once the building would have collapsed.

Grief is like that. There are stages we go through. Denial, anger, bargaining, depression, acceptance. Though not always all, nor always in the same order, they deliver us from what was lost to what will be. You will not get over the losses in your life until you have grieved. More precisely, you may never get over your losses, but you can get through them.

Job asked a big question early in this story: "Shall we accept good from God, and not trouble?"[280] The psychological

---

[280] Job 2:10

goal of grieving is acceptance but the road to acceptance has a few stops along the way. Job's story is a guidebook for grief.

Denial

After cancer, I hoped to recover, but I never recovered the man I had been. I didn't deny having cancer. I denied the change that was happening within me. My inability to flex with the change eventually shattered me and my paradigms. My fixation on what I wanted be—no, on what I *should* be, only extended the process. I kept denying what was happening.

Job may not have denied the facts of his loss, but he denied the emotions of them. He wished he had never been born.[281]

Anger

When the reality of our loss sets in, anger starts to burn.

A year after I left his mother my youngest son came to Whistler and we skied and boarded the late spring snow. I was weary by early afternoon. Aaron did a couple more runs on his own. As we walked to the car with our gear over our shoulders two young women approached us and asked for our lift passes.

"No," I said.

"But you're not going to use them," the first one said and fluffed her hair.

"I live here and support local business," I said.

"Don't be selfish," the first girl said, and the other chanted "Bad karma, karma, karma."

I flashed with wrath.

---

[281] Job 3:1-4,11

"Why don't you go fuck yourselves!" I yelled.

I had never said anything like that! My regret was immediate and deep. It wasn't about the girls. They were just the occasion, not the cause. My failures and losses had simmered and boiled inside me long before that.

Job tore himself to pieces in his anger.[282]

That's what happens when we can no longer reconcile the experience of our lives with the absolutes we were taught. "Shall the boundaries be moved because of you?"[283] Job's friend asked. When the stable things are shaken something has to give. One going through grief can't be expected to hold it all together. If we are to be refined like gold, we can expect to turn into a molten puddle before the impurities float out.

Bargaining

"If you take a step of faith in the right direction, God will give you the strength to continue."

That was the good advice a professor, mentor, and expert in spirituality gave me. I reasoned that my life would be better if I did the right thing. But it didn't work that way. Each of the several times I took a step back toward my wife one of my retinas detached. It could have just been the stress.

Job didn't bargain with his future, but the past.[284] He insisted that he didn't deserve what he got. Life is not about what we deserve.

Depression

When Job realized that all his losses were real, when his anger was unrelieved, when his pleas made no difference,

---

[282] Job 18:4
[283] Job 18:4 a.p.
[284] Job 31:1-40

Job became predictably depressed. While his friends pressured him to admit he must have done something wrong, told him to change his bad attitude, Job wore four of the faces of depression.

Disillusionment

"What I do makes no difference. God does whatever he pleases and he's probably got more in store for me. God has made me lose heart."[285] Grief may be God's path to deliver us from false hopes, but we are incredibly vulnerable there. I believed my goodness had made no difference. Maybe a bit of badness wouldn't either. That's when I failed.

Comparison

When Job compared himself with others he saw that the poor suffer and the wicked thrive. Don't tie your hopes to fairness. Neither life, others, nor God are fair. When Job compared his life with the past, he longed for the good old days when God watched over him.[286] Ironically, God and the angels were watching him more closely in his grief than ever before! The meaning we attach to adversity can drive us into depression.

Despair

Job called, but God didn't answer. He stood up to get God's attention, but God merely observed. Job despaired of God's goodness.

> You turn on me ruthlessly;
> with the might of your hand you attack me.
> You snatch me up and drive me before the wind;
> you toss me about in the storm.

---

[285] Job 23:13-16 a.p.
[286] Job 24:1-12; 29:1-30:31

I know you will bring me down to death.[287]

"Do you have thoughts of ending your life?" my psychiatrist asked when things were at their worst. I couldn't sleep. Couldn't see from one side. Couldn't work. Didn't know what to do. Ran out of money.

"I won't end my life. But I've let God know that I'd be grateful if he did."

Defensiveness

After relentless accusation, Job got defensive.

"If I had mistreated women or my employees, or if I hadn't been generous with the poor; if I had gloated over my enemies or mistreated the land, I would understand my suffering," Job said. "But I haven't."[288]

Job was not defensive in the sense of someone who is excusing or rationalizing their failures. Job really didn't deserve his suffering. Ironically, my own fixation on the injustice of being pushed from the church prompted my own moral failure. There are times to defend ourselves, to fight for ourselves, but defensiveness, justified or not, is a roadblock to moving beyond depression. As long as the focus is on what we have or have not done, it is difficult to get our eyes on what God is doing. It's hard live with the need to be right, and to grow too.

Stuck In The Stages Of Grief

I have seen people stuck in the stages of grief. It is possible to be angry or depressed for decades. I myself have been unable to "get over it" for long stretches. In a culture that tries to be so persistently positive, it is hard to embrace

---

[287] 30:21-23
[288] Job 31:1,13,16-21,29,38-39 a.p.

the difficult paths to progress. What is it that moves us from one stage of grief to the next?

Honesty moves denial into anger; we need to remember what was lost.

Introspection moves us from anger to depression.

Acceptance follows depression not when we see circumstances differently, but when *we see ourselves differently*.

Humility moves us from depression to acceptance.

Acceptance Is The Goal Of Grief

God showed up and Job finally got what he wanted—sort of. God "spoke out of the storm."[289] That's when our lives turn; when God shows up.

The answer for grief is not an explanation. An explanation does not restore hope. Would you feel better if someone told you your tragedy was a challenge God chose to put on with the devil? We persist in offering information that doesn't touch the real problem in our search for comfort. Hope is not because we have all the facts nailed down. Nor is it rooted in what is likely. Trust may be based on performance, but belief is rooted in personal knowledge. Faith is the outcome of a divine encounter. We will not accept our loss and relinquish our concern for meaning and justice except to someone we know to be greater than us and our world. If we need more faith, we need more of God. God is not the One who provides the answers. God *is* the answer.

When God showed up he didn't offer answers to any of Job's questions. God started asking questions.

---

[289] Job 38:1; 40:6

Brace yourself like a man;
I will question you,
and you shall answer me.
'Where were you when I laid the earth's foundation?
Tell me, if you understand.
Who marked off its dimensions? Surely you know!'[290]

God asked Job about the creation of the earth, the light of the sun and moon and the placing of the stars. "Do you control any of these?"[291] Hippos and crocodiles are brought into the discussion. "Tangle with one of them and you'll never forget!"[292]

"Who then is able to stand against me?"[293] God says.

I saw hippos, crocodiles and elephants on my first foreign journey. After my second year of Bible College I went to Burkina Faso to witness and preach with the missionaries. I was immediately set to carpentry work instead; I built screens for windows, repaired furniture and set metal roofs over patios.

After a month we took an excursion. At our first stop we cruised a lake in an old metal boat left behind after World War II. We paused where a group of hippos floated with their nostrils and ears protruding from the water. Suddenly, one of the seemingly docile beasts charged the boat. Every fifteen feet it surged up out of the water, opened its giant jaws wide and roared.

---

[290] Job 38:3-5
[291] Job 40:15-41:34 a.p.
[292] Job 41:8 a.p.
[293] Job 41:10

"Hippos kill more people than any other animal in Africa," the missionary said.

The hippo swam below the surface again before emerging, louder, and closer to the boat. It swam beneath us and I wondered if the next surge would capsize us. We moved away.

Back on the red-dirt road away from the lake, the car stopped. Up ahead an elephant had pushed against the trunk of a tree until it fell across the road. The leaves had been beyond his reach. We waited.

Our last stop was a land-locked pond where crocodiles were worshipped. There were no fences or walls. There were no crocodiles in sight either. They might have been in a cave that burrowed into the clay bank at one end of the pond. Or they might have been resting in the verdant reeds that covered one side of the pond.

We bought a local chicken and hung it from a branch of the tree that shaded the entrance to the lair. Nothing stirred. A young man with a short staff approached us and after a few words with the missionary he strode into the reeds and swung the stick before him like a scythe. He had not gone far when a croc three times longer than he was tall thrashed and churned the water. The crocodile undulated and clawed its way to the cave with astonishing speed. The only thing faster was the stick-man running in the opposite direction with his arms and knees pumping the air! The world is different when it is not in a cage.

Have you considered these creatures? God asked.

Why was God intimidating Job after bragging on him through the story of his trials? God wasn't. God's great strength is not meant to discourage Job from friendship with God but to encourage him to trust in God's ability to deal

209

with any problem no matter how strong or fierce. What is beyond our strength and control is not beyond God's. God's display of strength and wisdom was not about intimidation. God was restoring Job's sense of awe; the combination of fear, wonder, and delight that we don't live well without. When I stand on a mountaintop or walk by the sea or stare at the stars, my sense of awe, and my place in the world, is restored.

Hebrew justice was less concerned with punishment than with a judge's ability to restore what the victim lost. God took the dispute beyond right and wrong by going to the matter of responsibility. God is strong enough. God never mentions the thieves who stole Job's life. He never mentions Satan either. What if there was no more need to blame? We can blame or we can grow.

When God revealed himself, Job accepted his life and losses.

> I know that you can do all things;
> no plan of yours can be thwarted...
> Surely I spoke of things I did not understand,
> things too wonderful for me to know...
> My ears had heard of you
> but now my eyes have seen you. [294]

Job didn't get the answers he was looking for. But he lost his questions too in his encounter with God. He found something truer. He found a hope that was beyond his circumstances; faith that transcended experience. Job came to know God.

---

[294] Job 42:1-6

I realized I had accepted my own losses while sitting in a coffee shop in Kelowna. The man I was waiting for was late and I was tired, so I put my head back against the coffee-shop wall and had a nap. When I woke, the woman a little farther down the upholstered bench was sleeping with a smile on her own face.

She opened her eyes, looked at me and said, "If you had moved down I could have stretched out and had a real nap!"

We both laughed and began to talk. She had previously lived in the small ocean-side town where I had lived. Somehow my cancer came out. Her husband had died of cancer six years earlier. I didn't often tell people I had been a minister, but I told her.

"Where?" she asked.

I gave a vague answer but she pressed for specifics. She wanted to know what the names of some of those I had worked with.

When I got to the name of the man who had orchestrated my departure from the calling and community I loved she said, "We never would have made it through my husband's cancer and death without that man's help."

I can believe that, I thought. *He always had an ability to connect with people.* My reaction astounded me. I felt no need to tell the woman about the man's failings, about the devastating effect his words and actions had on me and my family. I was free!

"Shall we accept good from God and not trouble?"[295] I have happily accepted that people are God's agents of

---

[295] Job 2:10

211

goodness. How did I think God would bring the trouble of his choosing to my life?

Beyond Grief

At the end of the book God affirmed Job, told Job's friends that Job knew Him better than they did, and said he would forgive their folly if Job prayed for them.[296]

Every sermon I preached has called for change from me. Week after week for twenty years I had to turn toward what God wants. It was often humbling and difficult. I need to do that now.

In my last meeting with the board of the church I poured myself into, the meeting where I resigned, each of the Board members said something to me. Some wept. Others apologized. Some showed nothing. At the end, one asked if I had anything more to say. I knew what he wanted. He was waiting for a blessing. They were pushing me out the door, without even being honest about it, and he wanted a blessing. At that time I felt like saying: *If you have dealt honestly with me, may others deal honestly with you. If you have deceived and undermined my life, may others deceive and undermine you.* I wanted to say that then. But not now.

I cannot say that I know God better than anyone else. I have not lived a blameless life. I have been hurt and I have hurt others too. All of this I accept.

I choose to bless now.

May God forgive our folly and turn us to our rightful minds.

May he restore the friendships that count.

---

[296] Job 42:7-9

O God, prosper your people so the work of their hands multiplies beyond all proportion to their efforts.

Be gracious to them and give them *peace*.

That was the name of the church: Pacific.

"After Job had prayed for his friends, the LORD restored".[297]

Conclusion

What can I say to someone who is at the end? I thought. Andrew was fiftyish, single, homosexual and dying on 10D; the Palliative Ward at Saint Paul's Hospital where I had volunteered years before to listen to AIDS and cancer patients. Andrew's sister was a dear friend and one of the kindest women alive. I had conducted their father's funeral a year before. Another brother had taken his own life decades before that. What could I say?

It needs to be about hope, I thought. But what can be said about hope when all the regular reasons for it have fallen like unpicked fruit? I found one verse in the Bible that seemed worthy of a man on the edge of life.

"Hope does not disappoint, because the love of God has been poured out within our hearts through the Holy Spirit who was given to us."[298]

I hadn't been on 10D for years, in those earlier days a patient named Samuel had a picture by his bed. The man in the frame was happy, healthy, strong.

"Is that your partner?" I asked.

"No," Samuel said, "That's me."

---

[297] Job 42:10
[298] Romans 5:5 NASV

The muscle was gone, the tan too. Occasionally a smile still surfaced.

Sam's family smiled a lot when they came to visit. His brother shook my hand.

"I'm an ordained minister too," he said.

"You're going to be okay, dear," Sam's mother said. "We've prayed and all you need is faith to be healed."

Sam's brother the ordained minister leaned closer and smiled seriously. I recognized that look. He was about to pray. They were loving him in the best way they knew.

"Mom," Samuel said, "This is it. I'm dying."

Her smile fractured and tears leaked through the cracks.

"We'll come back when you're feeling better," she said.

After they left, after the time it took to settle, Sam said, "Shit falls away from you when you're dying."

It need not be the final death to deliver us from our delusions. The little deaths that come to every life can deliver us too. True hope lives on the other side of the clichés we have held to. There is hope that has little to do with the expectation of good things.

The Buddha understood the need for a different hope when he said life is suffering, and yet found enlightenment. Victor Frankl understood that as a prisoner in Nazi concentration camps when he said hope lies not in asking what we expect from life, but what life expects from us. Jesus lived this when his life was not taken, but given.

Our hope is not in our circumstances. Hope is not a calculation of facts and arguments. Hope is a relationship. Hope is within us; God with and in us. The Bible says we have this hope within us because God has poured his love into us by his Spirit. "And hope does not disappoint."[299]

After an hour of conversation with Andrew on 10D I asked, "Do you know that God loves you?"

Italy was my cure for grief. Six years after leaving the church, after losing my community, my marriage and my vision, I breathed in the inspiration of Roman art and architecture and history. In a year without obligation I rose when I woke, ate when I was hungry, and learned to tango with my sensual and warm Italian friends. I found a rhythm of meditation, writing, and inspiration. Breathe out... Breathe in... Fresh air. Fresh Spirit. It was not just the change of circumstances but of perspective that transformed me.

Einstein's train with two men provided new perspective. I found a fresh perspective when I was thrown off an Italian train.

I needed two tickets. The first for a commuter train from Bolzano to Verona, and a second for the high-speed train to Roma. My host helped me get the right tickets and then we lingered over lunch. I stepped on to the train just before it left. Not ten minutes later the green-jacketed conductor came down the aisle and checked each person's ticket. When he got to my row I handed him my two tickets; they were stapled together.

"This must be validated," the conductor said.

"*Scusi?*" I asked.

"You must validate this ticket before you get on the train," he continued in English.

"Can you validate it now?" I asked.

---

[299] Romans 5:5 NASB

"No," he said. "It is an open ticket that you could use at any time. Now you must pay if you wish to stay on the train."

"I did pay. I just bought the ticket an hour and a half ago."

"You must pay," he said. "Equal treatment for all. You could use this ticket two months from now."

"I will be in Canada two weeks from now. How much?"

"Fifteen Euros."

The ticket had only cost eight.

"You want me to pay three times for a ticket I already bought?"

"Equal treatment for all," he said again.

"In Italy?" I asked.

That was when I stopped worrying about doing everything right and wondered instead how the story would turn out. My motto that year was *Stand Up*. This seemed like an ideal opportunity.

"If you do not pay I will call the Carabinieri. You can get off the train at the next station."

The worst that could happen would be a conversation with two military police. They would wonder why they were talking to a Canadian tourist about an eight Euro ticket he didn't know enough to have stamped before boarding the train. Beyond that there might be a night huddled on a bench in an unknown village. More likely someone would take me in. The Italians are hospitable people, certain train conductors excepted.

"When is the next train?" I asked.

"An hour."

I would miss my connection in Verona and that closed ticket cost forty-eight Euro. I took out my wallet and pulled out fifteen Euro.

"No," the conductor said, "Fifty."

"Fifty," I repeated. He took the ticket from my hand and put it in his breast pocket.

"What is your name and your employee number?" I said.

"My name is Roberto…" he began and then covered his employee badge. "What is your name?" he asked.

"My name is Gregory Schroeder and I am a writer and you are going to be famous."

I took back the ticket from his pocket as he told me I would be getting off the train at the next station. The girl across from me told me I could validate the ticket and jump right back on. But as soon as I stepped off, the conductor blew his whistle and the train pulled away. The platform was empty but I checked the schedule. The next train left in twenty minutes. He had lied to me about that too in the hope that I would miss my connection. I made it with two minutes to spare.

Prudence is good, but life is not meant to be lived like a manual (this step follows that step… see diagram 3a…), but like a story! When I read a novel and a page is full of crisis or conflict I don't close the book in dismay or fear, I turn the page! What happens next? There is a reason why two thirds of the Bible is narrative. Not only books, but life, is better approached this way. Mystery overtakes dread. Fear is replaced with anticipation. Even a troubling story doesn't extinguish hope. It provokes it!

Why are we so afraid to step off the train? Are we afraid to be left behind? It is possible to step in again.

Out Of The Box

In Greek mythology Prometheus stole the secret of fire from the gods. Zeus was so angered by the loss that he commanded Hephaestus, the god of craftsmanship, to create the first woman. Hephaestus molded her from earth and water. Aphrodite gave her beauty. Apollo gave her music and Hermes gave her the gift of persuasion. Everything was added to her life until she was "Pandora," one who had everything to offer. Then, before she was sent to live among mortal men, she was given one more thing; a jar, with the instruction to never to open the lid.

Prometheus warned his brother Epimetheus about gifts from the gods, but Prometheus married Pandora all the same. It was the gift of her own curiosity that prompted Pandora to open the jar and out spilled toil and grief and every other evil. Pandora tried to put the lid back on but it was too late. There was just one thing left in the jar. Hope.

The story reminds me of a perfect garden named Eden with just one *Do Not Touch* sign. That day ended with a chapter of loss and one line promising deliverance.[300] It would be a long wait until God sent someone who broke out of the box.

After searching for a month, I found the ending to this book on the curb of the Stanley Park seawall. Whatever it was, it was eight inches high and wide and deep. Carved patterns curved and climbed the burgundy cube to a flat top with a gold painted cross. I knelt and looked around to see who might have left it. There was no one.

The box was wet. I picked it up and took its weight; it was too light to be solid, so I looked for a latch, for a door.

---

[300] Genesis 3:15

As a boy my parents gave me a puzzle box that was impossible to open until I learned to tug and slide three panels in the proper sequence. Standing on the seawall I looked for a secret entry to the wooden box with the cross on top. I rapped my knuckle on each side, on top, and on the bottom. The paint was chipped and the corners had been battered. This box dripped with the sea. It had been beaten on the rocks when it came to shore. My fingers ran over the edges and my eyes scanned the seams.

The bottom was thinner. Hollow. Did it hold something? I pulled on a piece of trim and the bottom slid open. The box was empty. But the satin lining told me what had been inside. The box was an urn, a receptacle for the dead. It had been filled with the ashes of a passed life. Even those were gone now.

I imagine the box sank with the weight of those ashes when it first fell into the sea. Who knows how the water tossed and washed the urn until all the grief had sifted and seeped through the cracks? Then the box had risen to the surface and found its way to shore.

My body has been beaten, my edges are battered. The turmoil of time has washed over me and left me calling from deep to deep. A decade after leaving the church the ashes of my past have washed out.

A week after finding the urn, late at night, I loaded the box with rocks, walked to the centre of the Lion's Gate Bridge, and stood at the railing. *Don't wait too long here*, I thought. *Someone will think you want to kill yourself.* I never needed to end my life; just the way I was living.

You can't put new life in a box built for the dead. I threw it back and watched until I saw a splash of white and heard a mighty crack as the box shattered in the darkness.

219

Afterword

Time may not heal all wounds, but all wounds take time to heal.

After ten years, in just a few days every one of my immediate family, including my former wife, will spend Christmas Eve together. The close friend from church called after a couple of years and invited me for a cold drink on a hot day. We don't keep in touch now, but the memories have become golden. The church has gone on and we talked about talking.

I am not what I was, nor yet what I will be, but I am grateful and happy for what is, now.
Gregory Schroeder
December 19, 2012

About the Author

Gregory Schroeder (B.Th., MCS), served as an ordained minister for twenty years. He was chosen in college as the student most likely to succeed as a pastor, and won awards in seminary for evangelism and spiritual theology. Meetings with extraordinary leaders around the world as well as encounters with cab drivers in Mumbai and Rwandan widows have distilled themselves into insights that create clarity and transformation for individuals and organizations. Gregory is a transformational consultant, speaker and writer, rides a Honda VFR 750 motorcycle and plays the violin.

Gregory also wrote *The Rest of Your Life: stories of rest and restoration,* while recovering from cancer.

For information about booking the author to speak at your event email info@integrowellness.com